MACHINE RENDERING II
THE BOOK OF IRON

Dopress Books

CYPI PRESS

CONTENTS

CHAPTER I:
SMART MACHINES
ROBOTS & MECHANICAL CREATURES

CHAPTER II:
ENGINEER MECHANICS
TRANSPORTATION & MACHINERY EQUIPMENT

LARS SOWIG

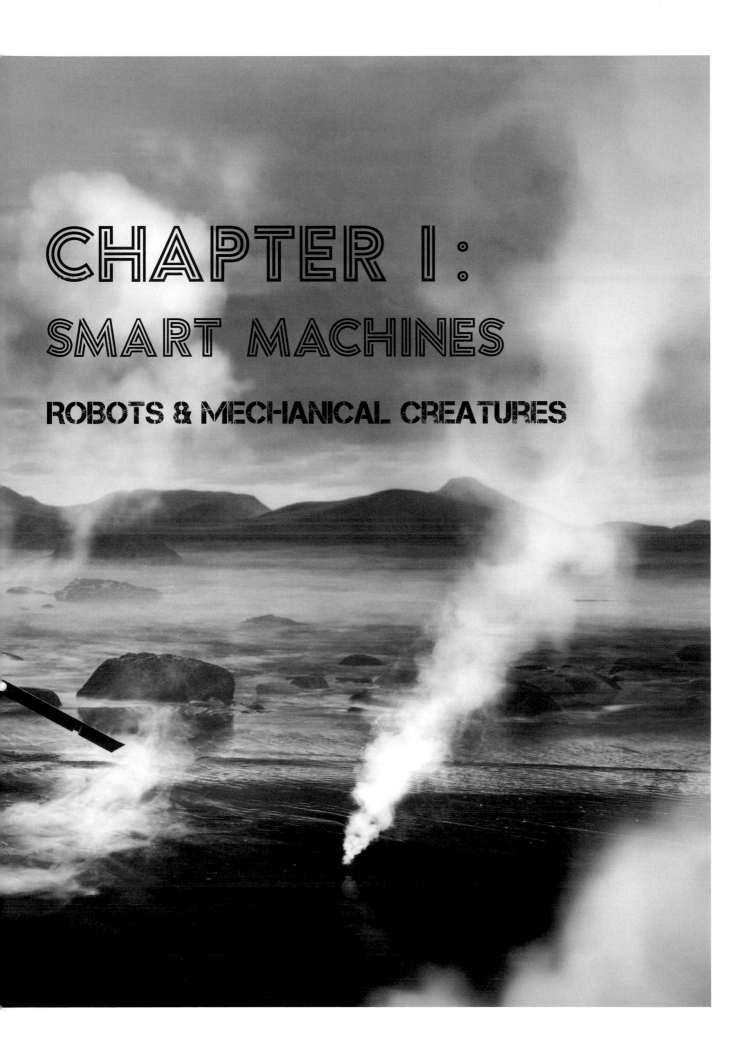

CHAPTER I:
SMART MACHINES
ROBOTS & MECHANICAL CREATURES

DANIEL HAHN [DAYTONER]

ABOUT THE ARTIST: Daniel Hahn, AKA Daytoner (DTNR for short) is a concept artist who does projects for games and movies. Currently he lives in Los Angeles; he moved there five years ago and loves it. He started sketching obsessively when he was about 15 years old and doing graffiti in his hometown in Germany, where he later studied product design.
MATERIALS AND TOOLS: ZBrush, Photoshop, KeyShot and Substance Painter
ARTIST WEBSITE: https://www.artstation.com/daytoner

WHEN DID YOU START CREATING MECHANICAL DESIGNS? WHAT WAS YOUR OPPORTUNITY TO START?

I am working as a product designer in the auto industry for a German manufacturer. When I was 16, I started to do graffiti in my hometown. I usually painted characters next to somebody else's letters. When I started working, I kept drawing characters and posing for fun. Mechanical design came as a perfect combination of my professional work and my passion. It combines product design, engineering and characters in one, which is why it's so much fun.

WHICH ARTISTS OR ART FORMS HAVE INFLUENCED YOUR CREATIONS?

During university I was heavily influenced by the Star Wars Episode One Artbook, and Syd Mead is one of my all-time favorite concept artists.

CAN YOU SHARE WITH US YOUR EXPERIENCE OF CREATING THIS KIND OF WORK?

My work is a chaotic mixture of different media. I am not perfect in the separate tools but I use each one to the point where it helps me communicate my ideas. I do sketch models in Zbrush, mostly to give me my proportions and lighting, and then I go over to Photoshop. I like photobashing a lot (collaging photos in Photoshop) as a base of my work. Once you start playing around with photobashing you will notice how quickly you come to ideas that you normally wouldn't have sketched on a blank paper. The downside is that you can get lost easily if you don't try to follow a concept in your head.

WHICH MECHANICAL DESIGN FROM A GAME OR MOVIE IS YOUR FAVORITE AND WHY? HOW DID THIS DESIGN INSPIRE YOU?

The latest movie I liked is actually a trailer called KELOID—if you don't know it you should watch it. The concepts are from Mr. Aaron Beck. I like the style of the robots because they look so brutally engineered and purpose-built. There are no faces and everything is put together from believable components. They could be built right now and there is no magic to the movements compared to the Transformers for example.

As for games, I'd have to go with Metal Gear Solid. Metal Gear Rex itself is dope but I also love the Geckos from MGS4 Sons of the Patriots. Such a good design for a walker. The mix between sheer metal surfaces and the organic legs is awesome.

1

1 *Blackops 1*

1 | 2
  | 3

1 *Blackops 2*

2 *Chameleon*

3 *Detonizer*

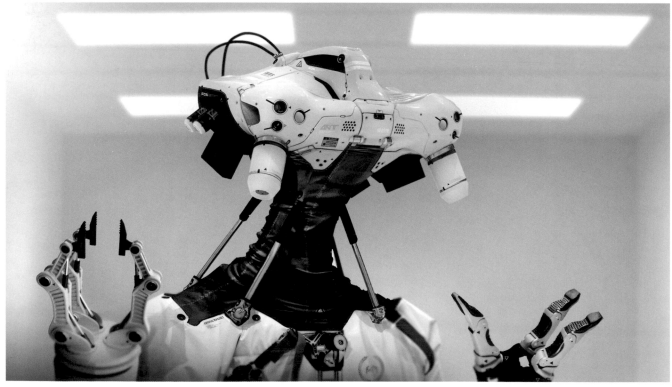

1 | 3
2

1 *Nine Eyes*

2 *The Plastic Surgeon*

3 *Stinger*

1 | 2
   | 3

1 *Master-Oni*

2 *Silencer*

3 *Doodes*

MARCO HASMANN

ABOUT THE ARTIST: Born in 1982, Marco Hasmann graduated in 2004 from the School of Comics in Milan, Italy. He worked for a decade in the comics industry, producing various publications for Vittorio Pavesio Productions, Star Comics, Studio 407, Soleil Editions and Redwhale. Under the supervision of Kawaii Studio, he also participated in the coloring of various Disney properties and graphic novels.
MATERIALS AND TOOLS: Photoshop, ZBrush, Substance Painter, Blender, KeyShot
ARTIST WEBSITE: https://www.artstation.com/hasmann

WHEN DID YOU START CREATING MECHANICAL DESIGNS? WHAT WAS YOUR OPPORTUNITY TO START?

I started making helmets and armour with the intention of contributing to one of my favourite games of all time: XCom. Most of this material has been done for my community mods: "Stenchfury Modular Helmets" and "Stenchfury Modular Armors." Aiming for a distinct objective can help keep focus.

OF THE SEVERAL TYPES OF MECHANIC DESIGNS, WHAT DO YOU THINK ARE THE DIFFERENCES BETWEEN THEM?

With each design I tried to explore different shapes that could still look good mixed with each other; the aim of the mod was to have interchangeable torsos, arms, legs, visors, helmets and masks. Of course the difficulty is to have something that could still look unique; the key is varying the main/big and medium shapes as much as possible.

CAN YOU SHARE WITH US YOUR EXPERIENCE OF CREATING THIS KIND OF WORK?

These helmets and armors were my first 3D works; at the time my workflow wasn't as technical as it is now. My main process was to build a very simple low poly mesh in Blender and make all the detailing work directly during the texturing process. Painting height and normal maps in Substance Painter is more controllable and faster when you are first approaching 3D; adding patterns and materials is extremely intuitive in that software.

WHAT WOULD YOU SAY ARE THE FEATURES OF YOUR WORK? HOW DO YOU FIND AND DEEPEN YOUR OWN STYLE?

I feel very close to the Concept Artist role; I always try to make something different while still getting inspired by old classics and more modern franchises. The key is to have a big background of references both in your mind and on your screen and the ability to make something that can look new but familiar at the same time.

Getting inspired by nature and other types of designs is also very important; you can add greater variety in this way. In terms of creating something that feels "new," it's important to look at stuff that seems totally different but that can still contribute positively to your design, like comparing to Transformers for example.

1

1 *Elephant Armour*
Dynamic pose shot for a portfolio piece; post-process done in Photoshop

1 | 3
2 |

1 *Elephant Armour*
Finished model after texturing

2 *Elephant Armour*
Another dynamic shot of the soldier in armor

3 *Gila Armour*
More dynamic pose shot

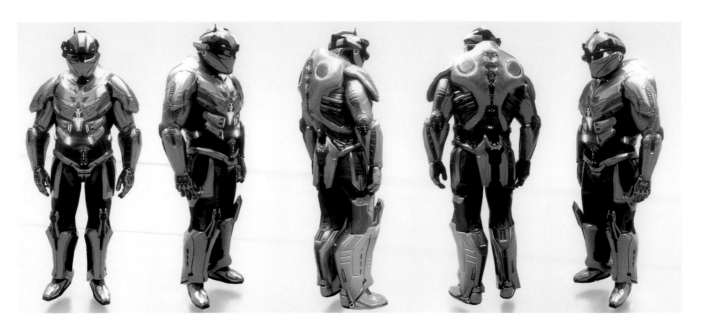

1 *Gila Armour*

Finished piece shown from different angles

2 *Gila Armour*

Set from a lower perspective, shiny parts
and emissives give a kick to the image

3 *Gila Armour*

Backpiece

1
─
2

1 *Typhoon Helmet*
   Fully detailed helmet after texturing process; glossy material and strong
   emissive give the shots more personality

2 *Typhoon Helmet*
   Final portfolio shot after post-processing in Photoshop

1

1 *Komodo Armour*
   Finished piece from various angles

MAX DMYTRIV

ABOUT THE ARTIST: Max Dmytriv is a UI/UX designer from Ukraine. He has six years of experience and started creating concept art and mechanical designs in his free time in the last two years. Max considers himself a newbie in the field and plans to continue his studies with 3D tools.

MATERIALS AND TOOLS: Photoshop and ZBrush

ARTIST WEBSITE: www.behance.net/MaxDmytriv

WHEN DID YOU START CREATING MECHANICAL DESIGNS?

I'm a UI/UX designer with six years of experience. I always wanted to create game art with some cool robots and monsters. Almost two years ago I started trying to create some concept art and mechanical design in my free time after work.

WHICH ARTISTS OR ART FORMS HAVE INFLUENCED YOUR CREATIONS?

I was really inspired by such awesome artists as Anthony Jones, Maciej Kuciara and Milan Nikolic.

WHAT TOOLS AND MATERIALS DO YOU PREFER?

Most of my concepts are painted in Photoshop; sometimes I use photobashing techniques, but recently I've started studying some 3D tools, such as Zbrush and 3D Coat.

WHAT ARE YOUR PLANS FOR THE FUTURE IN MECHANICAL DESIGN?

I'm just a newbie in this field and I still have a lot to learn, but I know that I can't become a real artist someday without using 3D, so I'm planning to continue my studies until I can call myself a concept artist.

1

1 *Robot (Police) Photobashing*
I used an image of a police officer and added details of bikes, machines, wires, then painted some details on top in Photoshop

1 │ 2

1 *Alien*

   I used Zbrush for the character concept, rendered in Keyshot and
   then added background and effects in Photoshop

2 *Invider*

   Character painted in Photoshop; for the background I used some
   photos

1

1 *Jet Fighter*

This image was fully photobashed, no painting or 3D; I used images of helicopters,
planes, bikes, weapons and combined them together in Photoshop

935 5686

YANEZ MEDINA

ABOUT THE ARTIST: Yanez Medina (Victor Hugo) is a professional graphic designer who works at a package design agency in Mexico City. He is also interested in illustration as a hobby, especially drawing robots and mechanical things. His main inspirations are his wife and daughter, music, travelling, taking photographs, watching airplanes and building model kits.

MATERIALS AND TOOLS: Pencil & paper, Wacom Intuos, Photoshop and Illustrator

ARTIST WEBSITE: https://ferkad.wordpress.com

WHEN DID YOU START CREATING MECHANICAL DESIGNS? WHAT WAS YOUR OPPORTUNITY TO START?

I started to draw mechanic design when I was at school. I always felt a fascination with robots and it was so exciting to watch anime in the 80s—it fueled my imagination, but at that time it was very difficult to find printed or any other type of references in my country. For that reason, I had to learn on my own about aesthetics and functionality of machines, understanding how they move and perform in a specific environment by reading and looking at books about tanks, aircraft and robots, and of course using a lot of imagination.

OF THE SEVERAL TYPES OF MECHANIC DESIGNS, WHAT DO YOU THINK ARE THE DIFFERENCES BETWEEN THEM?

There are many different types of machines and robots; mainly they are divided into fantastic machines and more plausible or realistic ones. But they are also divided into automated, programmed or intelligent ones and those that are controlled by a human. I have always liked mechanical machines that are controlled by a human. Artificial intelligence seems like a dormant danger for humanity. Machines are made by man so it is important to understand the motivations of man to understand why machines are created. They serve a purpose and the design responds to that specific task for which it was made.

WHICH ARTISTS OR ART FORMS HAVE INFLUENCED YOUR CREATIONS?

Some of the artists that have left a big impression on me are Shoji Kawamori, Mamoru Nagano, Makoto Kobayashi, Yoshitaka Amano, Metallica and Frank Herbert, among others. Macross, Five Star Stories, Gundam and other anime movies from the '80s are my main influence. When I was a kid I wanted to draw mechas like those I saw on TV; the level of detail and realism that the Japanese artists have is amazing, very inspiring. Macross started everything for me; I was captivated. I am self-taught; I learned about mechanical design by watching anime and studying the details in books from animation like Gundam.

WHAT ARE YOUR PLANS FOR THE FUTURE IN MECHANICAL DESIGN?

Until now all my work has been personal, but I really would like to work as a concept artist for video games, books or movies. I want to work making mechanical designs and concepts instead of just making them as a side project in my free time. And while I look for an interesting project, I am learning to explore each robot through different views and parts and trying to speed up my working process.

1   1   *The Manticore*
A mass production light combat mech with many variants for fighting, training, exploration and weapons testing; some variants are also called Sirocco but are basically the same machine

1 *Nasarok-Nuevo-Final*

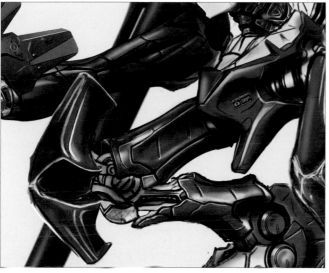
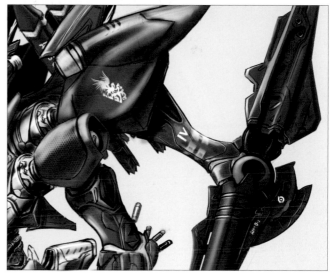

1 | 2

1 *Svart Draken*
A heavy combat mecha, designed to engage in combat with 2 or 3 enemies simultaneously; for that reason it was made with four arms, so it can handle twice the weaponry compared to a similar machine

2 *Svart Draken*
Step diagram

Иулюс Mk. II

1 | 2

1 *Mechanical Combat Armour for Infantry Troops*
2 *Step Diagram of Mechanical Combat Armour*

Хулио - Металл Человек

JULIO
EL HOMBRE
DE METAL

Иулюс Mk. II

TRYLEA

ABOUT THE ARTIST: As a teacher at the China Academy of Art, Trylea is an independent illustrator, concept designer, animation director, and director of animation art and game art. His artistic style conveys imagination and creativity; representative works include the Tmall logo, a series of illustrations of Chu Yun Zhi, and the animation Manjianghong. He won the 3rd Breakthrough International Illustration Competition of China and was champion of the 3rd China Illustration Contest.

MATERIALS AND TOOLS: Photoshop and pencil

ARTIST WEBSITE: trylea.zcool.com.cn

WHEN DID YOU START CREATING MECHANICAL DESIGNS? WHAT WAS YOUR OPPORTUNITY TO START?

Probably in kindergarten, because my school was far away from my home, so I could only watch the cartoon songs on my way home. In desperation, I did simple designs by myself on paper. When I was in elementary school, models became popular, and every time I looked at their package covers, I loved them. At this point, the brush met my hobby, and all kinds of armoured mechanical graffiti appeared in my textbooks. When I was in college, mechanical creations slowly turned from an amateur hobby into an expert pursuit, so I started using a digital board to make a series of mechanical creations.

WHICH MECHANICAL DESIGN FROM A GAME OR MOVIE IS YOUR FAVORITE AND WHY? HOW DID THIS DESIGN INSPIRE YOU?

What I like most are films directed by Neil Blomkamp, including District 9, Elysium and Chappie. Both with the visual design and the storylines, these films all show the director's strong personal style. The slum setting, the intensification of social contradictions, the cold metal armour textures, close to the real era, the study of artificial intelligence, species and class—all of these bring to us a very shocking sense of reality. From this point of view, I think that in the creation of mechanical art, we need to start creating from a specific point in time and space based on the real world, so as to design works that can move people's hearts.

WHAT WOULD YOU SAY ARE THE FEATURES OF YOUR WORK? HOW DO YOU FIND AND DEEPEN YOUR OWN STYLE?

Oriental steam punk—a lot of people like to describe my design work like this. I'm accustomed to combining traditional elements or elements of the times into mechanical creations. In my early creations, I started with architecture, incorporating some of the architectural visual elements into mechanical creations. The Buddha and the classical Oriental style temple are also a source of my inspiration. My process is to interpret some Oriental elements, and then use steel material to recreate my own works.

1 | 2

The Rebellion of Heaven: Sky

天机之乱
REVOLUTION OF SKYSTRATEGY
DIRECTED BY TRYLEA

1 | 2
    3

Transformers

H:10M
W: 30T
FORCE: 1032
NUM:002Z-TEST
DRIVE-CRY.UH

NICOTINE

ABOUT THE ARTIST: Nicotine is a senior concept designer, signing artist at Games Workshop (Warhammer, 40K), and art consultant at NetEase Games. He founded DRock-Art Studio, where he currently serves as CEO. He has been involved in a number of large-scale international game projects such as Dark Blood II, 40K, The Elder Scrolls, Warhammer II and Eternal Tower of Heaven. His works have been included on the CGHUB home page and in the Editor's Picks Archive.

MATERIALS AND TOOLS: Photoshop

ARTIST WEBSITE: https://www.artstation.com/artist/nicotine

WHEN DID YOU START CREATING MECHANICAL DESIGNS? WHAT WAS YOUR OPPORTUNITY TO START?

In my childhood, I was very good at composing various kinds of mechanical models with building blocks. An unintentional encounter with the Star Wars movie made a great impact on my childhood view of the world, and I began to create mechanical works in various forms, including models, painting and so on.

WHAT TOOLS AND MATERIALS DO YOU PREFER? WHAT ARE THEIR FEATURES AND HOW DO THEY HELP YOU WITH YOUR WORK?

Photoshop is often used in peacetime, and sometimes I also use 3D software, so as to better express the relationship between structure and shape.

WHAT ARE THE CHARACTERISTICS OF THE MECHANICAL WORKS YOU HAVE CREATED? HOW DO YOU FIND AND DEEPEN YOUR OWN STYLE?

I am good at various types of mechanical design, better at the near future and biological mechanical styles. Most often I will get inspiration from some specimen fossils. Nature is our best teacher, and can make you have a lot of unexpected discoveries.

WHAT ARE YOUR FUTURE PLANS FOR THE CREATION OF MECHANICAL SETTINGS?

At present, we are creating an original science fiction project, "The Boundary Apocalypse" which incorporates rich science fiction design elements. I hope to work with more designers to create a view of a science fiction world of great impact and imagination.

1

1 *Eyes of Democracy*
The new federal type II mechanical guard is the new security officer of the new Federation. They always pay attention to the dynamics of the new federation, every planet and every city

$$\frac{1}{2}$$

1 *Ark*

   The new federal defense class displacing ship, with total length of 996 meters, width
   of 460 meters and height of 230 meters. Carries full load of 12,400,000 tons, cruise
   11,600,000 tons, holds 2,300 people, has 4 "core X" reactors

2 *Trident*

   The new federal democratization displacing ship, with total length of 689 meters,
   width of 195 meters and height of 136 meters. Carries full load of 1,800,000 tons,
   cruise 1,500,000 tons, holds 120 people, has two sets of power type VI light-weight
   fusion reactors

1 | 2

1 *Thorne Empire Iron Curtain*
   Production of the tenth generation of Thorne Empire
   soldier walking armour, designed as a crucial force in
   heavy battle; named "iron curtain" because of its heavy
   armour and a full range of protection performance

2 *Edge Clamp*
   The new federated "prism" mechanic is an important part of the new
   federated mechanized force; they are combat engineers and technical
   engineering experts. The first focuses on temporary maintenance and
   modification of mechanized vehicles, tactical engineering operations
   and electronic warfare processing during battle; the second ensures
   the normal operation of mechanical vehicles, base maintenance and
   engineering support during non-combat

IVAN LALIASHVILI

ABOUT THE ARTIST: Ivan Laliashvili is a concept artist and illustrator who studied at the Academy of Fine Arts in Saint Petersburg, Russia. Ivan is currently working as an artist in the video game industry and resides in China and Russia.
MATERIALS AND TOOLS: Photoshop CS6, ZBrush, 3D Max, 3D-Coat and KeyShot
ARTIST WEBSITE: http://ivanlaliashvili.deviantart.com/
https://www.artstation.com/artist/laliashvili

WHEN DID YOU START CREATING MECHANICAL DESIGNS? WHAT WAS YOUR OPPORTUNITY TO START?

From a very early age I loved different mechanical machines. I was reading different kind of photo albums and art books about industrial design, car and vehical design. And I especially liked huge machines and trucks, like mining trucks, coal mining machines, scrapers and others. I have continued to create, draw and model them until now. I very love that these huge machines have different complex elements and details. And how all these separate parts work together as a whole.

WHICH ARTISTS OR ART FORMS HAVE INFLUENCED YOUR CREATIONS?

I couldn't name anyone especially. There are so many great and extremely talented concept artists and industrial designers. They all help me a lot in my daily work. But I think the most important thing is to study and learn from real life, from the things that are around us in our daily routine. Great sources of inspiration for me could be design books, photos of different kinds of mining equipment, etc.

WHAT TOOLS AND MATERIALS DO YOU PREFER? WHAT ARE THEIR FEATURES AND HOW DO THEY HELP YOU WITH YOUR WORK?

When I create any design I always begin with a small scratch or concept. Normally I simply use pen and paper. After that, I begin my work in 3D programs and applications, and finally I go to Photoshop and create the final art piece. I like that final work looks like a high-quality illustration, not just 3D render.

WHICH MECHANICAL DESIGN FROM A GAME OR MOVIE IS YOUR FAVORITE AND WHY? HOW DID THIS DESIGN INSPIRE YOU?

My favourite is the mechanical design in Ridley Scott movies. I think he has a great art sense. Any spaceships or machines from his films always look awesome!

1
—
2

1 Space Engineers 2

2 Space Engineers 4

1

1 *Homefront: The Revolution*

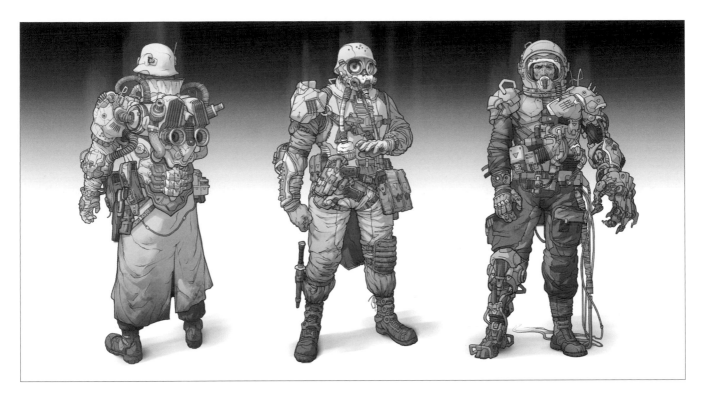

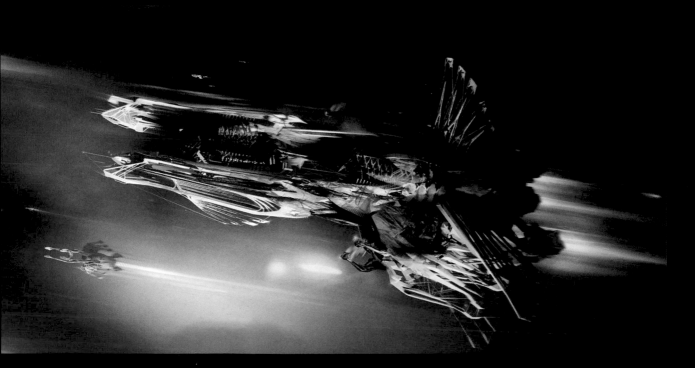

$$\frac{1}{2}$$

HENG Z

ABOUT THE ARTIST: Born in 1991 in Fujian, Heng Z is a professional conceptual designer. He was "crazy" about robots since he was a kid and began doing some of his own designs during university. After graduating in 2014, he found his first job and met a mentor who taught him design theories and techniques.

MATERIALS AND TOOLS: Photoshop

ARTIST WEBSITE: https://www.artstation.com/zz-heng

WHEN DID YOU START CREATING MECHANICAL DESIGNS? WHAT WAS YOUR OPPORTUNITY TO START?

Because I always loved to watch robot animation, then I naturally loved a variety of mechas. The real start of trying to design a mechanical setting for me was actually after graduating and working in a 3D animation company. A powerful mentor taught me conceptual design, and I had good luck. The tutor was a master of mechanics.

WHICH ARTISTS OR ART FORMS HAVE INFLUENCED YOUR CREATIONS?

Sparth, Brian Sum, Shinkawa Yoji and so on. I like their works very much. Their designs are very inspiring for me. I will think over their works repeatedly.

AS A CONCEPT ARTIST, HOW DO YOU PREPARE FOR A NEW WORK? WHAT ARE THE NECESSARY PRINCIPLES?

The first step for me is to consider the composition. That is to say, from the perspective of sketch, it should be a good-looking and interesting structure, and then consider the rationality of other aspects, and the general concept of the design should be in your mind. To prepare for the design, I think we should find some corresponding reference works. After all, a person's thinking is limited. Looking at other excellent works can provide more ideas for the artist, help him to pursue divergent thinking and complete the design.

WHAT ARE YOUR PLANS FOR THE FUTURE IN MECHANICAL DESIGN?

I hope to design some more unique mechanical settings, and a series will be taken into consideration. I am still exploring my own style and always trying to improve my works.

1

1 *Armoured Design: Reference Halo Style*
Latent combat armoured suit with electronic jamming device and a magnetic force system

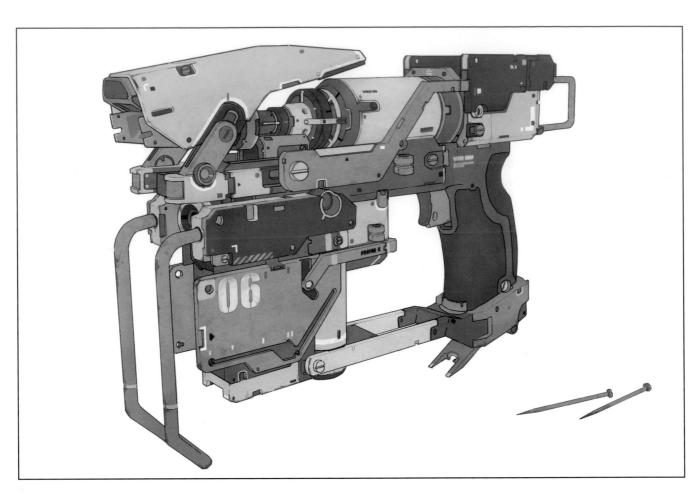

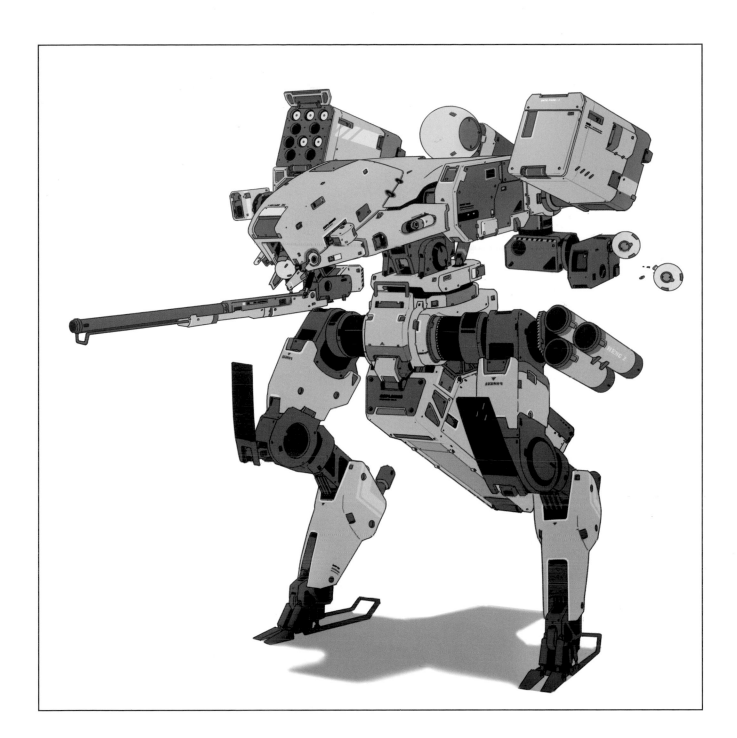

1
2
3

Transformers

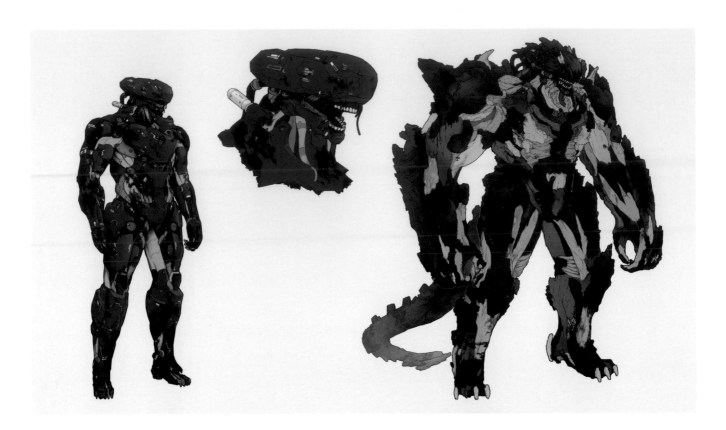

1 | 3
2 |

Transformers

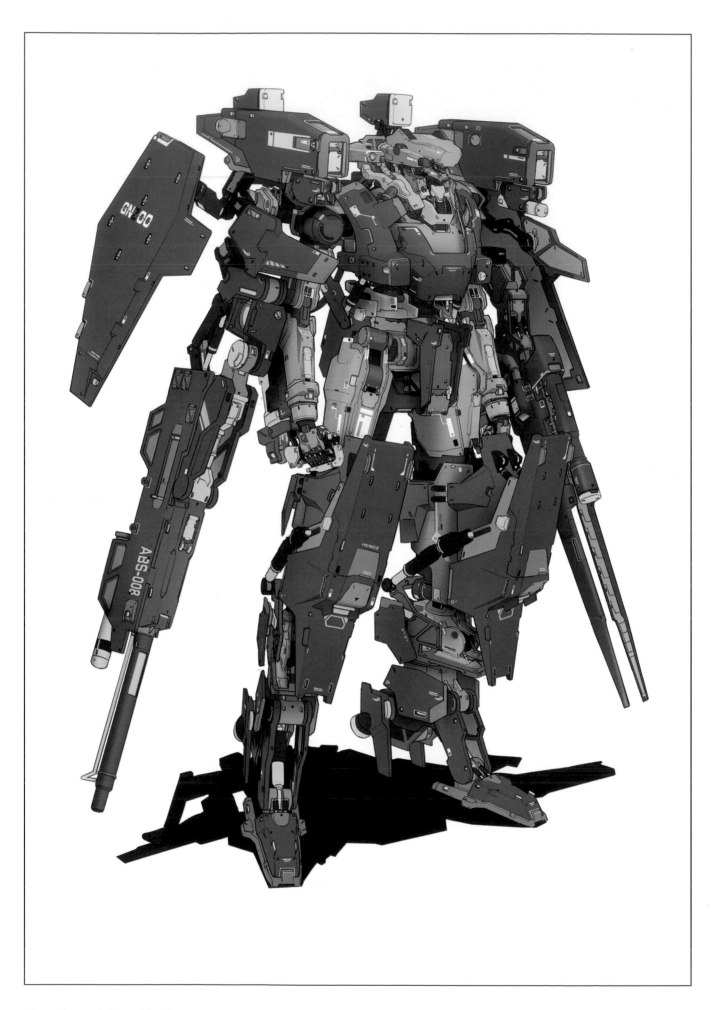

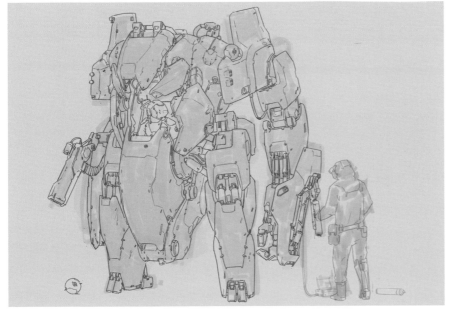

1 | 2
3

Transformers

GUIMING

ABOUT THE AUTHOR: Since 2011, Guiming has been engaged in graphic design work, and is currently focused on the design and development of catering brands. He loves music, games and movies; his inspiration comes in large part from movies, especially sci-fi wars of history, and from hip-hop and electronic music. He also likes street culture related to hip-hop, such as graffiti and skateboarding, and is trying to blend some street elements into his futuristic designs.

MATERIALS AND TOOLS: Model painting tools

ARTIST WEBSITE: http://www.zcool.com.cn/u/642067

WHEN DID YOU START CREATING MECHANICAL DESIGNS? WHAT WAS YOUR OPPORTUNITY TO START?

I was very interested in machinery and the military since I was young. When I first saw Gundam in junior high school, I was deeply fascinated by this robot. I began to try to make robot models. In 2007, I chose the animation profession, dreaming that one day I could design my own robot.

WHICH ARTISTS OR ART FORMS HAVE INFLUENCED YOUR CREATIONS?

There are many artists who have influenced me, such as Ano Hidea, Mamoru Oshii, Neil Blomkamp and so on.

WHAT TOOLS AND MATERIALS DO YOU PREFER? WHAT ARE THEIR FEATURES AND HOW DO THEY HELP YOU WITH YOUR WORK?

I usually like to use some special model painting tools. With the progress of the times, these tools are becoming more and more convenient. Such progress provides more possibilities for the artist's creativity and saves a lot of time and production costs.

WHICH MECHANICAL DESIGN FROM A GAME OR MOVIE IS YOUR FAVORITE AND WHY? HOW DID THIS DESIGN INSPIRE YOU?

My favorite is the Gundam series, which have fewer details than some new machinery now, but they look so cool. The inspiration to me is that when you design an excellent mechanical setup, you shouldn't assume that it will be eliminated from the aesthetic with the progress of the times. You can gradually upgrade and improve on the original foundation.

1

1 *Body Coating Mechanical Warriors*
In the Gundam series, using the old effects

<table>
<tr><td>1</td><td>3</td></tr>
<tr><td>2</td><td>4</td></tr>
</table>

1/2 *Transformers*

3/4 *Code Name "Unicorn" Model RX-0*
     Body of a mechanical warrior in the Gundam series

Transformation of Camouflaged Body
Prototype from the Gundam Series

1
2
3

Segesta

Prototype from the Gundam Unicorn, inspired
by the Milky Way escort

1 | 2   *Sniper GM*
  | 3   Prototype from the Gundam 0080; I designed
              a textured coating for the body

FAN CHEN

ABOUT THE ARTIST: Fan Chen graduated from Savannah College of Art and Design with a master's in industrial design in 2014. He was passionate about concept design and began to teach himself conceptual design and get freelance design work while still in school. After graduation, he worked in interior design of business aircraft in the US before returning home in 2015. Since then, he has studied conceptual design and engaged in business design work including scene design for screenplays, model design, mascot design and logo design; but his main focus is conceptual design of sci-fi mecha.

MATERIALS AND TOOLS: Photoshop, Wacom

ARTIST WEBSITE: https://www.artstation.com/artist/fanchen1989
http://chenfan.zcool.com.cn/

WHICH ARTISTS OR ART FORMS HAVE INFLUENCED YOUR CREATIONS?

In my earliest contact with conceptual design, I looked at some Massive Black tutorials. But the real introduction for me was Zhu Feng's "design cinema" series. He always stresses the importance of the line manuscript, of the proportion of the picture and of perspective. These are the basic principles of the "design" itself. Image rendering, color, and others are all based on these. In addition, he emphasizes the design idea, and accumulates more design inspiration and material. For example, in science fiction, we must start with science fiction, science and technology itself. Learning the knowledge in reality can make it more realistic in the future.

WHICH MECHANICAL DESIGN FROM A GAME OR MOVIE IS YOUR FAVORITE AND WHY? HOW DID THIS DESIGN INSPIRE YOU?

I really like the concept of the film District 9. The aliens, weapons, the walking armour and the story in the movie really impressed me, and the design style of the film is very unique. The problem of combining machinery and organisms often encountered in science fiction was also done very well. This film is one of my favourites. The design of the film "Guardians of the Galaxy" is also among my favourites, especially the armour and weapons of the raccoon character. The role itself is very attractive. All these have inspired my creation of animal and machine designs.

AS A CONCEPT ARTIST, HOW DO YOU PREPARE FOR A NEW WORK? WHAT ARE THE NECESSARY PRINCIPLES?

People have a potential sense of the proportion of objects. For example, a top-heavy design or one with an unstable barycenter will make people uncomfortable. In fictional objects, especially mechas where the human body is closely connected to the objects, those real objects can't break the rules. Unlike the design of realistic objects, the purpose of conceptual design is to open ideas. The last is setting style. What kind of background and the design language should be in designer's mind first.

1   1   *The Chase on the Bridge*
May be influenced by a similar scene in the Transformers film

1 | 3
2 |

1 *World War II-Style Jugger Naught*
  Uses World War II Soviet tank armour elements, like rounded edges and
  sturdy appearance, plus the star and emblem as the most prominent logo

2 *Extraterrestrial Truck*
  A vehicle seemingly for the shape of the colonies; intake on the front end
  suggests there is oxygen on the planet

3 *Skull Face Armour*
  The color looks older and there is graffiti on the body. The two-bar artillery of
  the arm still represents its fighting and killing nature

$$\frac{1}{2}$$

1　*Ancient Armour*
　A man accidentally discovers a long-hidden ancient giant mecha. Uses stitching techniques, to make the painting process faster and simpler

2　*The Mecha Cat Series*
　This is a cat character under the story of the armour set. The combination of organism and artifact is very interesting; the organism is not the common human form, but the cat. I specially drew the cat at the side of the figure to control him

ELIJAH MCNEAL

ABOUT THE ARTIST: Elijah McNeal is a freelance concept artist in the film and video game industries. Elijah has worked on titles such as Gears of War 4, Lawbreakers, Paragon, Fortnite and League of Legends, among many others.

MATERIALS AND TOOLS: Photoshop, Medium, ZBrush and 3DS Max

ARTIST WEBSITE: https://www.artstation.com/artist/el1j4h

AS A CONCEPT ARTIST, HOW DO YOU PREPARE FOR A NEW WORK? WHAT ARE THE NECESSARY PRINCIPLES?

I often look for a theme. What is the situation? Is this a military, engineering, medical, or other professional operation? Often it's one of those situations. I will quickly do some sketches, either 2D or 3D, to lay down my ideal shapes and determine a language. The final stage is to justify its function and existence. The principles I find necessary are exposing yourself to what you love doing artistically. Studying the fundamentals of design as well as art are paramount to increasing your skills. It is much more about doing than it is about thinking.

OF THE SEVERAL TYPES OF MECHANIC DESIGNS, WHAT DO YOU THINK ARE THE DIFFERENCES BETWEEN THEM?

The shapes and functions of the designs. You could have ten spider tanks in front of you, and these may all feel drastically different by their shape or even their purpose, but the basic function is the same. There may be ten different objects with a different purpose, but a similar shape could make them look as if they are all the same thing with the same function.

WHAT WOULD YOU SAY ARE THE FEATURES OF YOUR WORK? HOW DO YOU FIND AND DEEPEN YOUR OWN STYLE?

Clear in intent with a sense of weight. I try to leave little to ambiguity as for what I'm designing, but I don't always finalize every detail. I want the viewer to engage their imagination to some degree. I think art is more powerful when it's something that you can digest easily while considering its flavor.

WHAT ARE YOUR PLANS FOR THE FUTURE IN MECHANICAL DESIGN?

I'm rather content with what I am doing at the moment, and quite busy. I do plan to bring a book to publication but it's still a project rather than a product at the moment.

1

1 *Archer*
This image is just an idea for a cyber enhanced character; she's an iteration of an earlier idea for a sci-fi elf assassin

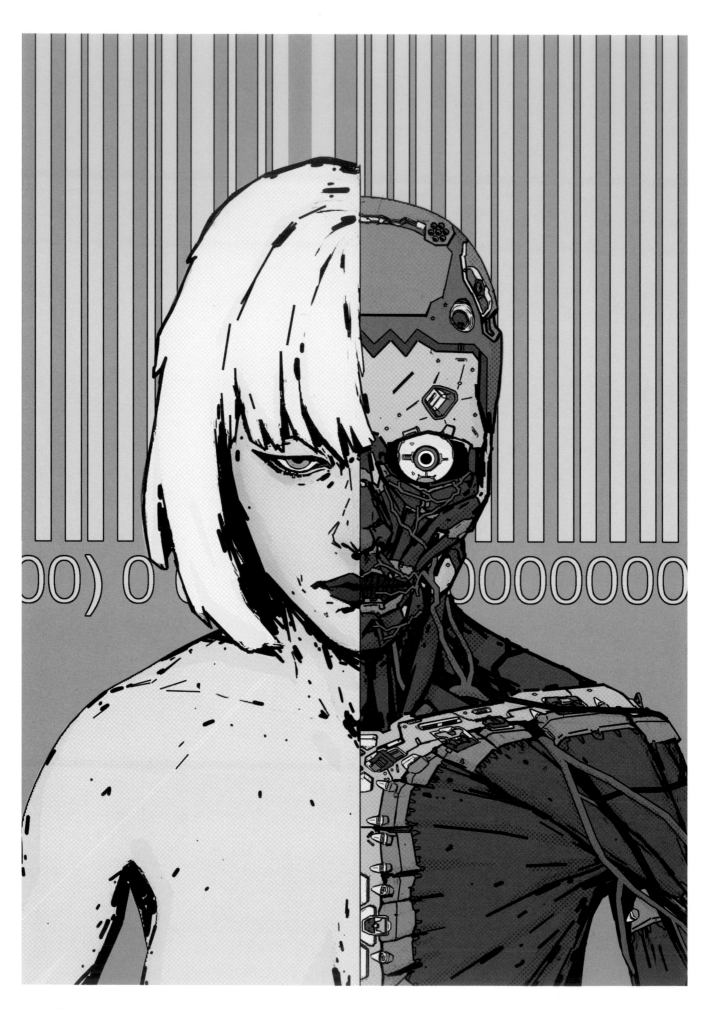

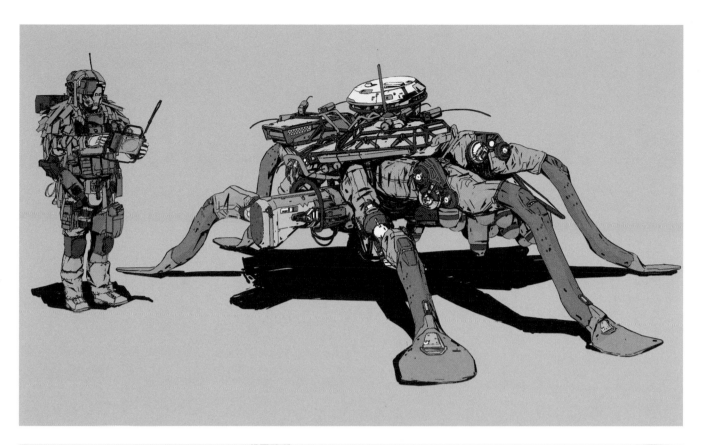

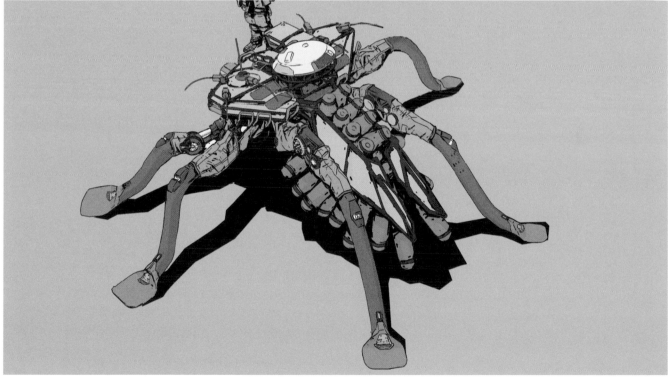

1 | 2

1 *Emily-Ecorche*

A cybernetic ecorche study

2 *Roach*

A strange creature used like the mechanical mules for the military; can carry
equipment or be strapped with a sizable payload, as in the image

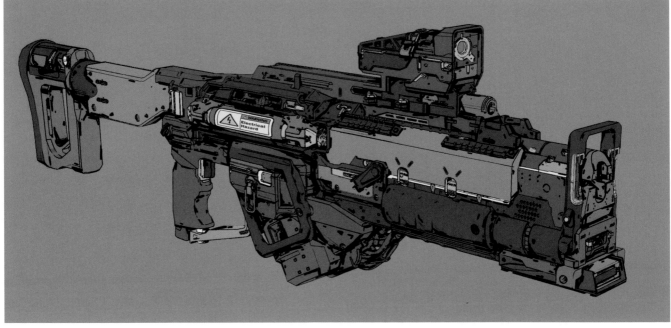

1
2 | 3

1 *Jade*

   This is the original elf character design I later upgraded into the stealth exo suit

2 *Electric Shotgun*

   A charged slug shotgun; the slugs are held in a high capacity drum that feeds
   the receiver. The charge is delivered through a battery cell that's discharged and
   reloaded, similar to rifles

3 *Wrex*

   This is an old character I've revisted a few
   times. It's a bit over the top, being a robot that
   also has an exo-skeleton attached

JUAN MANUEL OROZCO

ABOUT THE ARTIST: Juan Manuel Orozco, also known as JML2ART, is a 25-year-old graphic designer and illustrator from Costa Rica. He grew up with crayons and brushes, and a passion for the world of art and illustration, as well as for the geek worlds of comics, movies and video games. He currently works in the clothing design industry creating posters, as well as for several companies that sell products and designs inspired by pop culture and the geek and gaming worlds. He is also a freelancer on many projects for musicians and other companies, etc.
MATERIALS AND TOOLS: Paper, Wacom Cintiq and iPad
ARTIST WEBSITE: www.behance.net/jml2art

WHICH ARTISTS OR ART FORMS HAVE INFLUENCED YOUR CREATIONS?

One of my favorite artists is Keith Thompson; I love his style with a lot of details and the complexity of the robots and mechanical pieces. Also I like Yutthaphong Kaewsuk, Dan LuVisi and Shōji Kawamori.

WHAT TOOLS AND MATERIALS DO YOU PREFER? WHAT ARE THEIR FEATURES AND HOW DO THEY HELP YOU WITH YOUR WORK?

When I started, I loved the traditional tools, but for speed and at the request of my clients, I use a Wacom Cintiq and obviously a lot of books for reference, investigation, etc.

WHAT WOULD YOU SAY ARE THE FEATURES OF YOUR WORK? HOW DO YOU FIND AND DEEPEN YOUR OWN STYLE?

The feature of my work is the number of details in each piece, and I love to play with a lot of colors and do complex combinations of colors; also my style is more vector illustrations than digital paintings.

WHAT ARE YOUR PLANS FOR THE FUTURE IN MECHANICAL DESIGN?

I want to keep growing as an illustrator, improve, and be recognized around the world.

1

1 *Dinosaur*
Artwork commissioned to
WazShop; this was the first
Dinosaur as a robot he ever made

1 | 2
  | 3

1 *Iron Man vs Ultron*

This fanart was designed with the release of the film Avengers: Age of Ultron, and was so fun and different to do

2 *Hustle Techniques*

This work was made for a DJ called Mooch, and he told me he wanted a detailed artwork inspired by the game Portal

3 *BAJUG Juniper Networks*

This piece was made for Juniper Networks in 2013 for the presentation of an intern project

1 | 2 3
  | 4 5

1   *Creation from the Tour 2016*
     Designed for DJ EXCISION, part of the touring exhibition

2/3 *Fan Art Inspired by the Movie Civil War*
     I wanted to do artwork inspired by the art nouveau style

4/5 *God Animals*
     My own creations, animals with a particular style full of
     details and colors

1 | 2

A Robot and Urban Ruins

HUAQING ZHAO

ABOUT THE ARTIST: Based in Dalian, China, Huaqing Zhao graduated from Tsinghua University as an industrial design major, and founded Paperman Design. He now works at a technology company in Beijing as a design director, and has participated in product development for the Chinese military. He's interested in designing products that are possible and impossible, and he's very passionate about the latest technology and rock music. His belief is that all designs are the same. He pursues material product design while at the same time pursuing the concept arts. His representative conceptual design work is Mech Zeppelin.

MATERIALS AND TOOLS: Rhino, 3D Max and ZBrush

ARTIST WEBSITE: https://www.behance.net/9123752442dbd

WHEN DID YOU START TRYING TO CREATE MECHANIC DESIGN? WHAT IS THE OPPORTUNITY TO START?

I tried to use new software to design product models when I was in university, and I studied ZBrush, which opened the door to a new world. Then I tried to use mechanical setting skills to make products, and to use product design ideas to make machine sets and amazing effects. So I went down the two roads at the same time.

WHICH ARTISTS OR ART FORMS HAVE INFLUENCED YOUR CREATIONS?

I especially like the Wat Rong Khun, designed by Thai architect Chalermchai. The large, complex group of sculptures made a huge impact on me, and later my design began to become more "monochromatic" and "complex."

WHICH MECHANICAL DESIGN FROM A GAME OR MOVIE IS YOUR FAVORITE AND WHY? HOW DID THIS DESIGN INSPIRE YOU?

I like the X police force, the reverse robot of the future. This is a parameterized design style similar to Zaha Hadid's architecture, which is quite different from the robot with strong sense of equipment. Later, I tried to do some similar concept settings, and found that there were a lot of similarities between the mechanical setting style and architectural design. When my mind is exhausted, I look at exaggerated interior decorations and buildings that will inspire me.

AS A CONCEPT ARTIST, HOW DO YOU PREPARE FOR A NEW WORK? WHAT ARE THE NECESSARY PRINCIPLES?

Pretty cool, is certainly the first one. Of course, it is best to integrate the styling and the story background. We need to use "design" vision and thinking to treat our works instead of just showing off painting skills and software skills. This requires the artist to have enough experience and imagination.

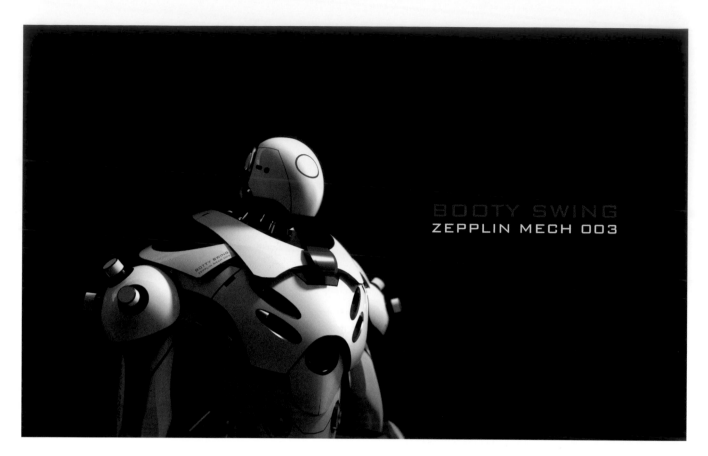

BOOTY SWING
ZEPPLIN MECH 003

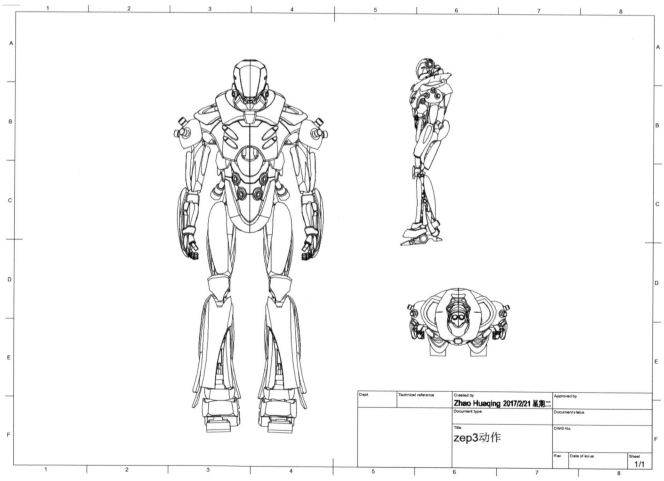

Dept.	Technical reference	Created by		Approved by	
		Zhao Huaqing 2017/2/21 星期二			
		Document type		Document status	
		Title		DWG No.	
		zep3动作			
				Rev. Date of issue	Sheet 1/1

1 | 2

1/2   *Booty Swing, Zeppelin Mech 003*
A security robot, loves music and
dance, and the golden age of rock-and-
roll in the 70s of the last century. He is
wearing pants—he dreams of being a
rock musician robot

HAPPY NEW YEAR
2017

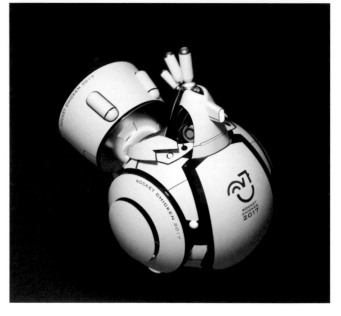

1 | 2

1 *Rocket Chicken, Zeppelin Mech 005*
   The chicken robot was designed to
   celebrate the Chinese Year of the
   Rooster 2017

2 *Moving Torch, Zeppelin Mech 001*
   A small robot with simple artificial
   intelligence, has been manufactured
   in large quantities as a geological
   exploration robot, but because of its low
   price and low intelligence, it is mainly
   used as a pet and lamp

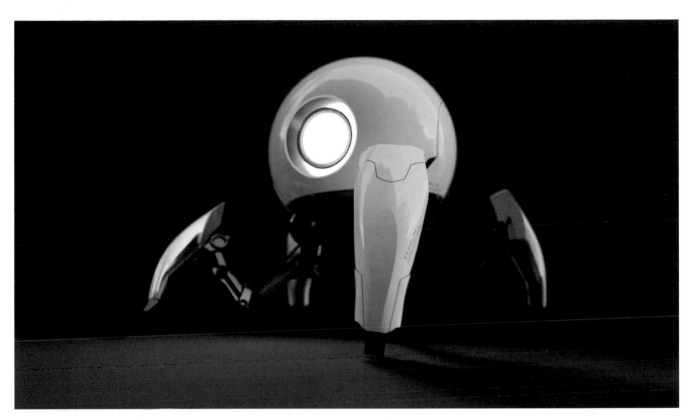

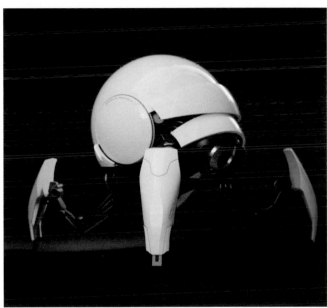

TANO BONFANTI

ABOUT THE ARTIST: Tano Bonfanti is an illustrator and concept artist who focuses on sci-fi and fantasy themes, and whose style includes a specialization in character design. Tano worked as an illustrator at 6pixel in Santa Fe, Argentina and as a concept artist at The Polymorph Extra in Shanghai.

MATERIALS AND TOOLS: COPIC markers & pens and digital tablets such as Wacom

ARTIST WEBSITE: https://tano.artstation.com; https://www.behance.net/tanoilustra

WHEN DID YOU START CREATING MECHANICAL DESIGNS? WHAT WAS YOUR OPPORTUNITY TO START?

I always loved mechanical things from a really young age, no matter which kind—planes, cars, motorbikes and of course androids and mechs. For me there is something really aesthetically interesting about the small shapes that mechanical objects have. I was also an architecture student in the past, so I was introduced to several machines from an early stage. The opportunities exist every day; you just need to decide if you are serious enough to sacrifice the time and effort to do this craft.

WHICH ARTISTS OR ART FORMS HAVE INFLUENCED YOUR CREATIONS?

Some of the most influential artists for me were Jean Giraud (Moebius), Feng Zhu, Daniel Simon, Frank Frazetta, Katsuhiro Otomo, Hayao Miyazaki and countless others.

WHAT TOOLS AND MATERIALS DO YOU PREFER? WHAT ARE THEIR FEATURES AND HOW DO THEY HELP YOU WITH YOUR WORK?

Most of the time I use my Wacom Studio Pro—it's a wonderful tool as it allows me to have the same sensitivity as pen and paper but in a digital medium. I also draw constantly with analog tools, like markers, pencils and pens.

WHAT ARE YOUR PLANS FOR THE FUTURE IN MECHANICAL DESIGN?

I think I will investigate more and more. I like to get more detailed every time, and try to emulate the real mechanics of machines that I like. This gives the illustration a realism that wouldn't exist if the mechanics were too weird. You have to put some true-to-life factors in the construction of the piece.

1

1 *The Android Taking Care of the City*

 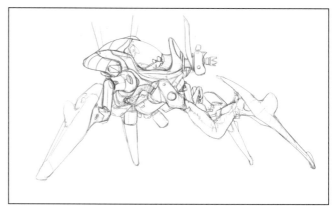

1 | 2

1 *Crab Mech*
2 *Character Design Line-up*

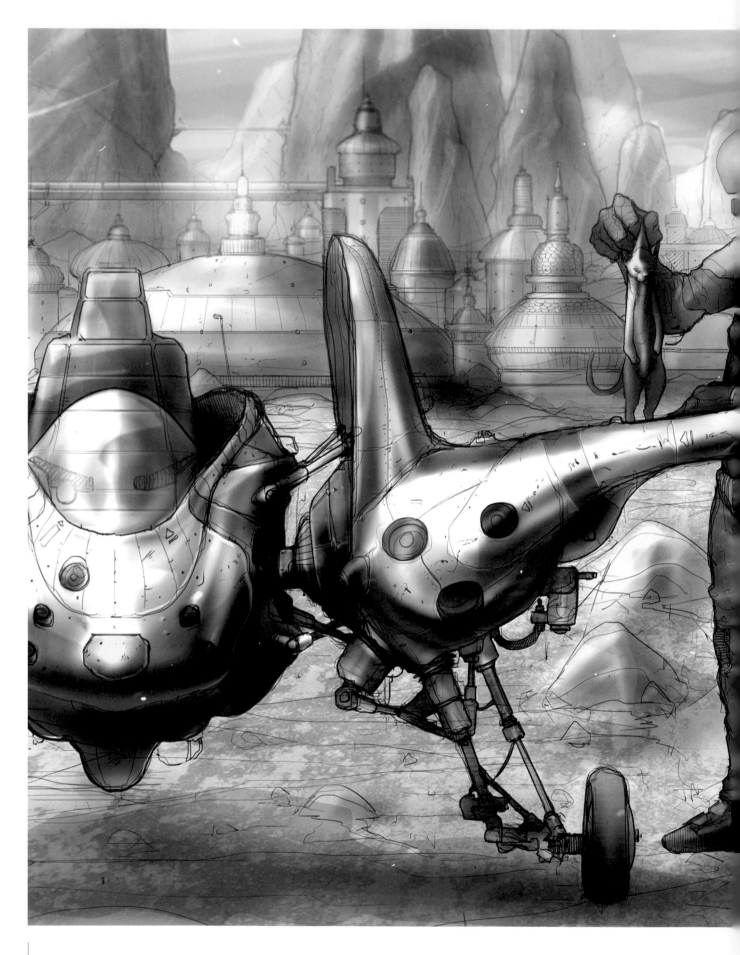

1   1 *Friends About to Fly*

LARS SOWIG

ABOUT THE ARTIST: Lars Sowig is a concept artist living in Neu-Isenburg, Hessen, Germany. He worked as UI/UX designer at Deutsche Telekom in 2015, where he received the German Design Award, then as UI/UX and Conception Designer at Honda Europe. He later worked as a concept artist at Crytek, where he received the German Game Award for Best Presentation 2017. Most recently he has worked as a concept artist at Massive Entertainment - A Ubisoft Studio.

MATERIALS AND TOOLS: ZBrush, Marvelous Designer, KeyShot, Photoshop and Illustrator

ARTIST WEBSITE: https://www.artstation.com/sowig

WHAT TOOLS AND MATERIALS DO YOU PREFER? WHAT ARE THEIR FEATURES AND HOW DO THEY HELP YOU WITH YOUR WORK?

I always prefer 3D input over building an image from scratch. Having proper 3D renderings as a base really helps to find the best working composition and also allows for presenting them from different angles. I have Keyshot in my Pipeline for quick material application and also quick rendering. It's super easy to use and provides me with helpful passes that I can then take in Photoshop. One important feature to mention here are Clown passes that provide me with a color ID map, based on my material distribution on my 3D models. These color ID maps help a lot in masking out areas in Photoshop and readjusting them.

WHAT WOULD YOU SAY ARE THE FEATURES OF YOUR WORK? HOW DO YOU FIND AND DEEPEN YOUR OWN STYLE?

As my work is all based on 3D, I feel like one main feature is that this 3D look remains in the final outcome. At the same time, I am making use of textures from the real world, which leads to a kind of cross-over between reality and 3D rendering. I also try to make my images look stylized and less real. I am mainly inspired by the Metal Gear series and the anime classic Ghost in the Shell, which defines my style.

AS A CONCEPT ARTIST, HOW DO YOU PREPARE FOR NEW WORK? WHAT ARE THE NECESSARY PRINCIPLES?

I think I have three main principles which are Research, Research and Research. This is really important as it not only sparks a lot of ideas and is key to the motivational factor, but it is also necessary to create believable designs and concepts. Besides gathering countless images, I also find it useful to spend some time doodling initial sketches based on that research to find a good direction.

WHAT ARE YOUR PLANS FOR THE FUTURE IN MECHANICAL DESIGN?

In the future I want to focus way more on functionality. This is absolutely necessary to create extra immersion and make things even more believable. An extra round of in-depth research would definitely support that.

1 1 *Disc*
Character concept for a robot with a thug personality

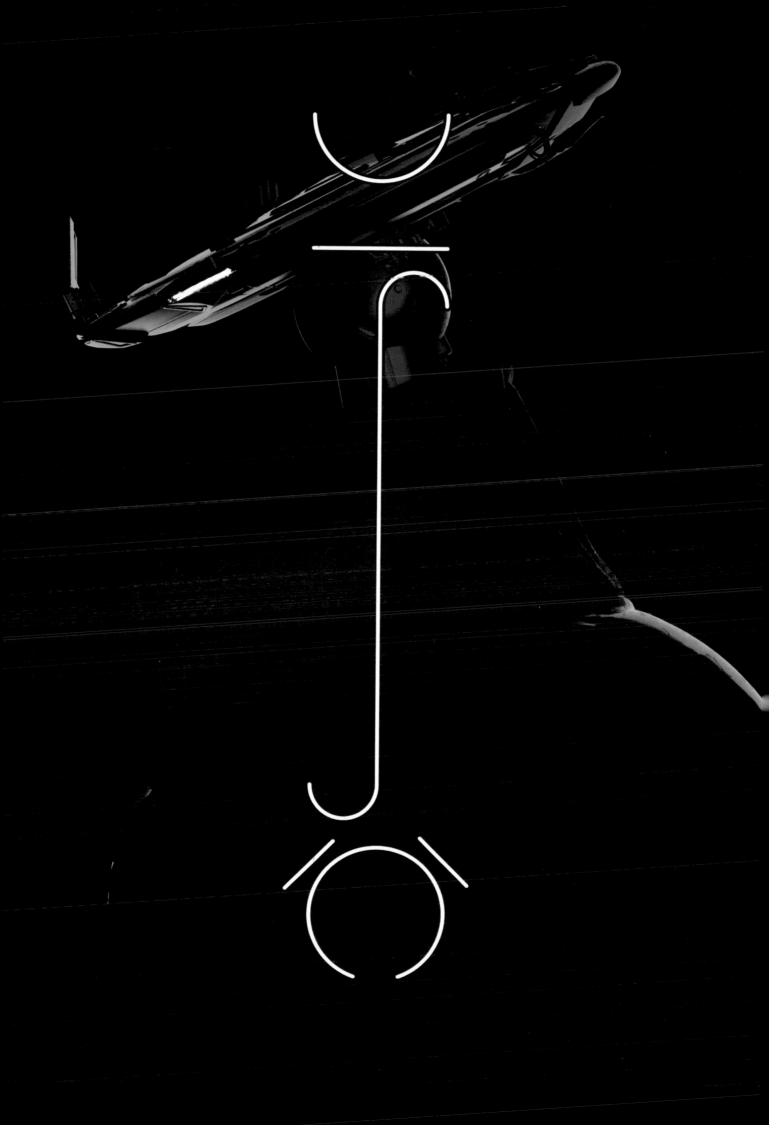

1
—
2

Disc
Character concept for a robot with a thug personality

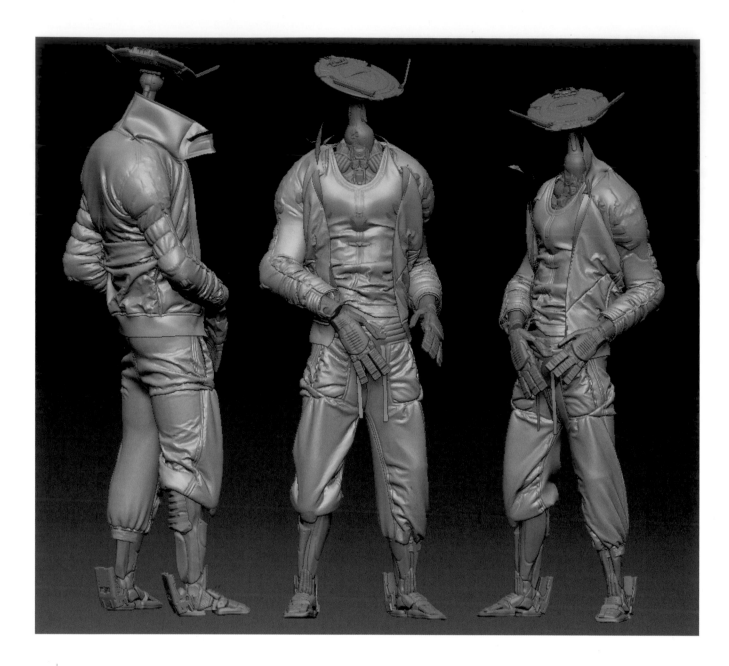

1 | 2
  | 3

1   *Disc*
    Character concept for a robot with a thug personality

2/3   *Disoriented*
    Visual development and mood concept for a dystopian,
    futuristic world where the line between humans and
    robots fades

1 | 3
2 |

1/2　*The Sirens*
Concept design for a space-conquering warrior
inspired by the ancient Greek hoplite soldiers

3　*Disc*
Character concept for a robot with a thug personality

CREATED BY LARS SOWIG

1   1 *Poseidon*

My interpretation, how I imagine a god of the
sea could look

CHAPTER II:
ENGINEER MECHANIC

TRANSPORTATION & MACHINERY EQUIPMENT

ALEXEY ANDREEV

ABOUT THE AUTHOR: Alexey Andreev is a visual artist, VFX supervisor, art director and concept artist working in a multitude of media including films, games and illustrations. He has a background in maths and classical sculpture. He now works for Blur Studio and lives in Los Angeles.

MATERIALS AND TOOLS: Maya, ZBrush, KeyShot and Photoshop

ARTIST WEBSITE: alexey-andreev.com

WHEN DID YOU START CREATING MECHANICAL DESIGNS? WHAT WAS YOUR OPPORTUNITY TO START?

My friend asked me to create some concept art for the game he was creating. At that moment I was a character artist and I accepted this challenge as it gave me an opportunity to upgrade my skills and learn some mechanics.

WHICH ARTISTS OR ART FORMS HAVE INFLUENCED YOUR CREATIONS?

I think Vitaly Bulgarov dominates the whole area of mechanical design at the moment. But I always try to find inspiration outside the entertainment industry. Modern military, robotics and prosthetic designs are amazing source of inspiration.

WHAT TOOLS AND MATERIALS DO YOU PREFER? WHAT ARE THEIR FEATURES AND HOW DO THEY HELP YOU WITH YOUR WORK?

Usually I combine 2D and 3D in my work. I create a rough base for my design in 3D software and then refine it in Photoshop. 3D gives you an opportunity to quickly explore the form and find proper proportions. I love to kitbash as it makes you move fast and you can get great details within an hour.

AS A CONCEPT ARTIST, HOW DO YOU PREPARE FOR A NEW WORK? WHAT ARE THE NECESSARY PRINCIPLES?

I try to explore the theme as much as possible and to find inspiration in different sources. This could be in art books with the works of grand masters, in scientific research from MIT or just in a book with nice photos. Of course, it all depends on the subject of the work. If the job is big enough I can spend hours and days on research. Usually it results in collection of images, or a mood board with key ideas for the project.

THE DRONES

1
—
2

1 *Harvester Drone*

2 *Scout Drone*

1   1 *Assault Tank*

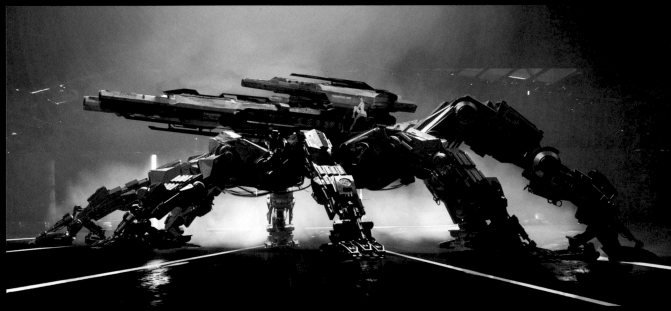

| 1 | 3 |
| 2 | 4 |

1 *Alien Creature*

2 *Hunter Drone*

3 *Moon Rover Concept 1*

4 *Moon Rover Concept 2*

EVGENY PARK

ABOUT THE ARTSIT: Evgeny Park is a self-taught 3D concept artist, a Korean born in Kazakhstan who now lives and works in Russia. He took his first steps into 3D at age 16 with a 3DS Max disc his sister gave him, but he abandoned it after a few months. At 18 he thought about a future career and decided to try 3D one more time with more passion; he says he never thought about what he might achieve until becoming confident enough to enter a contest for the first time and winning. His unexpected success served as a trigger for Evgeny to continue his design work.

MATERIALS AND TOOLS: Modo and Photoshop
ARTIST WEBSITE: https://www.behance.net/KLICKSTOP

WHICH MECHANICAL DESIGN FROM A GAME OR MOVIE IS YOUR FAVORITE AND WHY? HOW DID THIS DESIGN INSPIRE YOU?

Horizon Zero at Dawn, Ghost in the Shell (anime and movie), Gears of War, Akira, Halo, Doom, Half-life and Dishonored are typical, though. Recently I found a cool comic book called Zombie VS Robots and it's full of awesome robots! It's inspiring when I see some regular forms in new and interesting combinations. I love looking at how real-life stuff works, like cars, computers and bikes, etc.

WHICH ARTISTS OR ART FORMS HAVE INFLUENCED YOUR CREATIONS?

To be honest, it's all about these awesome guys Tor Frick, Vitaliy Bulgarov, Ash Thorp, Maciej Kuciara, Gavriil Klimov and others. But it's not only about artists, actually. Sometimes I walk with my friends in the industrial district, taking pictures of construction vehicles like some asphalt pavers, or old cars and other stuff. It's normal in Russia to find old mechanical equipment on the streets… it's just everywhere.

WHAT TOOLS AND MATERIALS DO YOU PREFER? WHAT ARE THEIR FEATURES AND HOW DO THEY HELP YOU WITH YOUR WORK?

For most of the model creation process, I use Luxology Modo. I really fell in love with this software and I think it has one of the best polygon toolkits. It also has a shader that can create round edges on the render in any part of the model, so you can see how this can speed up the overall creation process! Also this software is easy to learn, too. Actually I do render in Modo too. If in my designs I need soft forms, I use Pixologic ZBrush and Photoshop for some basic post-processing of my shots.

AS A CONCEPT ARTIST, HOW DO YOU PREPARE FOR A NEW WORK? WHAT ARE THE NECESSARY PRINCIPLES?

Today when you can follow works of other great artists, it's easy to fall into imitation. When I had just started my first steps in concept design, I often just repeated others' techniques and design principles. I watched hundreds of tutorials and modelling principles, but now after all of that I have developed my own design rules. They're not entirely new, but I made them by myself so I believe that I do have some sort of individual style.

1   1 *Front Detail View*

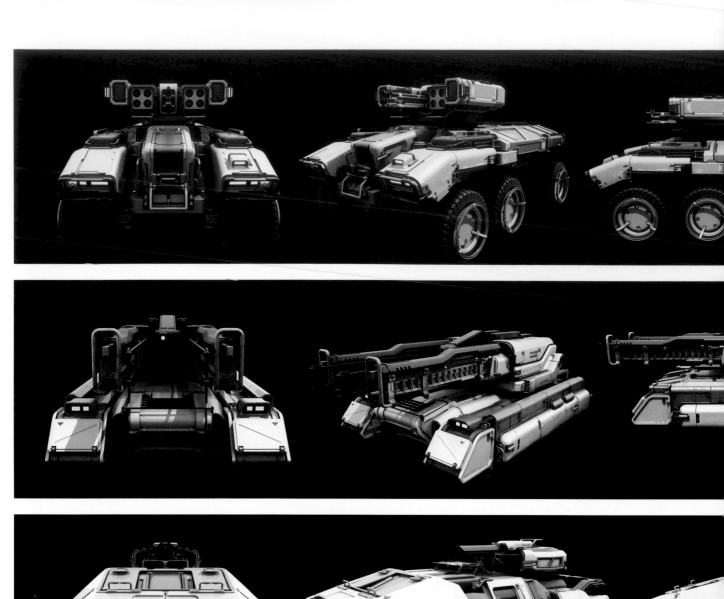

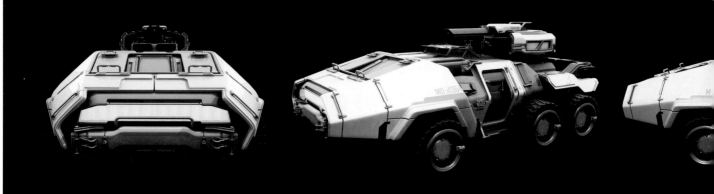

1   1   *"Concept Vehicles" Project for Dairy Free Games Studio*
When the model was ready and approved, I made a simple color palette review, then added small decals such as logos,
some division numbers and other stuff. In the final stage, I rendered all this with a simple light scheme

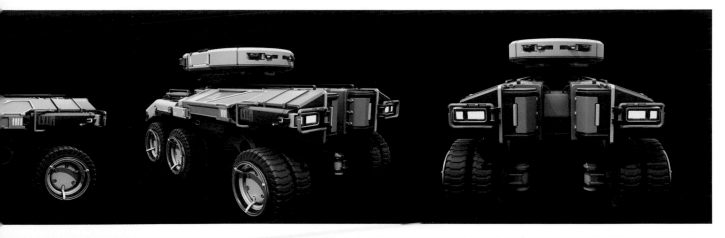

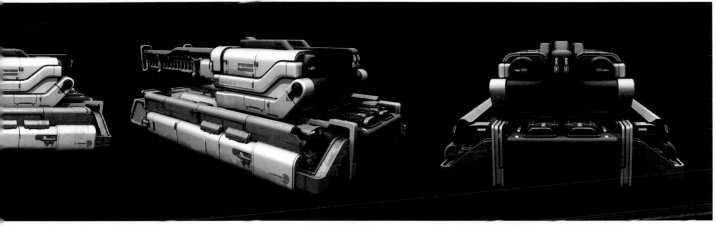

1   1 *Front Shell View*

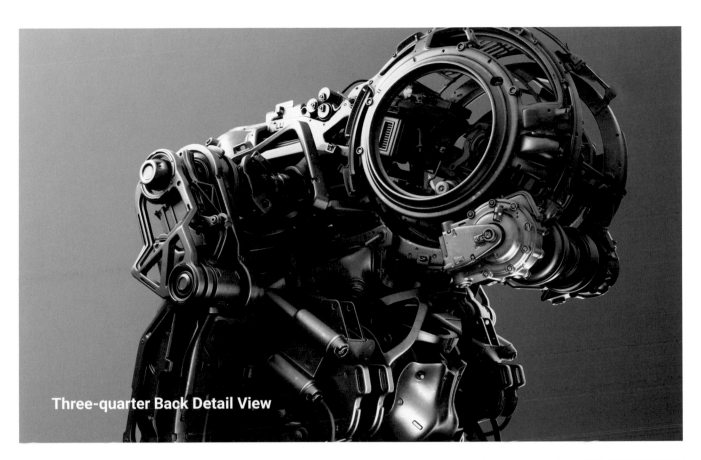

Three-quarter Back Detail View

Three-quarter Front Detail View

1	3
2	4

Details From Different Perspectives

RESEARCHER

1 | 2

The main task for this design was to be able to fly in both
space and atmosphere, and it had to carry a crew of up to
15 men. In terms of shape, it had to look minimalistic and
fast, more like a sports car with small details

ARTURO RAMIREZ ACOSTA

ABOUT THE ARTIST: Arturo Ramirez Acosta is a self-described happy father and husband, as well as a freelance creature and character artist. He has been working as a freelance 3D artist for over three years, and is now working for HuevoCartoon (Mexico) as a Look Development Artist.

MATERIALS AND TOOLS: ZBrush, Maya, KeyShot, Arnold, Substance Painter and Photoshop

ARTIST WEBSITE: http://www.artstation.com/artist/limkuk

WHEN DID YOU START CREATING MECHANICAL DESIGNS? WHAT WAS YOUR OPPORTUNITY TO START?

I started creating mechs one year ago. I was freelancing at the time, and after that I really liked creating biomech suits as well as mechs, so I can say that whole world is really amazing to me. The opportunity to start is every moment, pick time of your day, 15 or 30 minutes a day and begin to practice. Every moment is perfect for creating. I study from a lot of robots and mechs in the movies as well as their concept art.

WHICH ARTISTS OR ART FORMS HAVE INFLUENCED YOUR CREATIONS?

Well, I admire three artists: Maciej Kuciara, Vitaly Bulgarov, and Marco Plouffe (Keos Masons). The forms that they create, these mechs that are both functional and beautiful, are freaking awesome, and that's the reason I follow their work.

WHAT TOOLS AND MATERIALS DO YOU PREFER? WHAT ARE THEIR FEATURES AND HOW DO THEY HELP YOU WITH YOUR WORK?

I use ZBrush to create the basic forms, 3D sketches and Hi Poly models with details, and to create poly-painting textures. I use Maya to create new topology and refine hard surface parts, also I use it to create shading and lighting, to get everything ready to create the final render with the AOVs to import into Photoshop. Mari helps me to create really nice projections of texture and to paint the other baking maps, Substance Painter to create the PBR materials, which can be for videogame models, and Photoshop to create the final comp and final concept, ready to present to the client.

WHAT DO YOU THINK ARE THE FEATURES OF YOUR WORK? HOW DO YOU FIND AND DEEPEN YOUR OWN STYLE?

Well, I really like details when I work, whether it's a creature or a mech. I think one thing that the people can say a piece is mine is my color palette. I almost always use cold colors with touches of pinks, reds and oranges. Also the lighting I think is another factor; I really like dramatic lighting. And another, I guess, is that I really love to create mechs or creatures without a mouth, I think that they look more mystical and interesting that way.

1   1 *Personal Project*

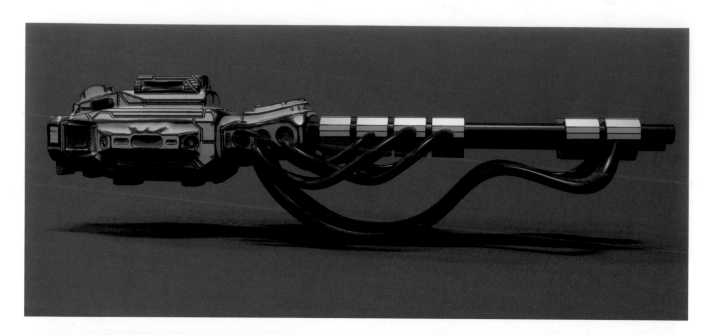

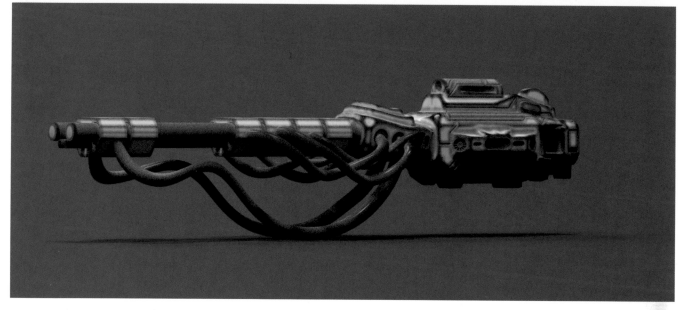

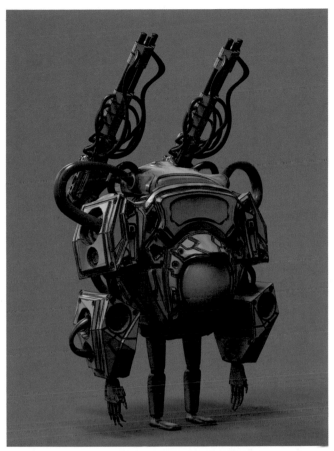
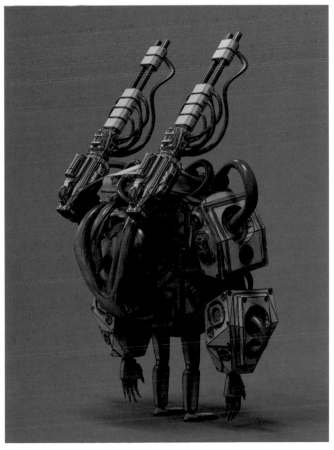
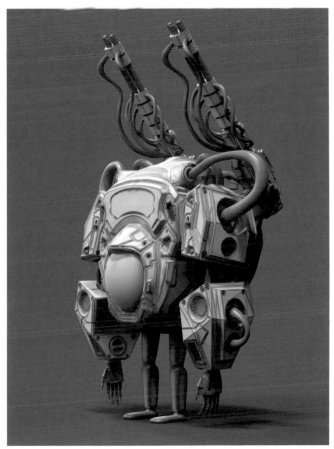

MAX EMSKI

ABOUT THE ARTIST: Max Emski works in the video gaming industry as a professional 3D artist with skills in hard surface modeling, texturing, UE4 and Unity3D rendering. He is also proficient in Autodesk Maya, Fusion 360, Foundry Modo, Substance Painter, Substance Designer, Arnold Renderer, Maxon Cinema 4D, Unity3D, Unreal Engine 4 and Adobe Photoshop.

MATERIALS AND TOOLS: Autodesk Maya, Foundry Modo and Arnold Renderer

ARTIST WEBSITE: maxemski.com

WHAT TOOLS AND MATERIALS DO YOU PREFER? WHAT ARE THEIR FEATURES AND HOW DO THEY HELP YOU WITH YOUR WORK?

I have tested many 3D applications over the last two years. I use Foundry Modo and Autodesk Maya, basically. Foundry Modo has great tools to simplify my work process at early stages. Besides that, this package includes all the necessary tools to create a project from beginning to end and get a high-quality final render. Modo has a user-friendly interface, a lot of tools and a huge quantity of free plugins, which solve all the possible problems with 3D modeling I might have. Modo's standard shader is amazing. This shader allows me to create very realistic procedure materials and textures without any additional applications. Navigation in Maya's viewport with more than 30-60 million polygons is easy as well, as in a scene with several cubes. Besides that, Maya is used by nearly all major game development companies and filmmaking companies, somewhere in their pipeline.

WHICH MECHANICAL DESIGN FROM A GAME OR MOVIE IS YOUR FAVORITE AND WHY? HOW DID THIS DESIGN INSPIRE YOU?

I really like sci-fi movies and video games. I'm inspired by games such as Alien Isolation, Deus Ex, Fallout and Mass Effect. I'm especially inspired by the environment from Alien Isolation, mechanical design from Deus Ex, and post-apocalyptic robots and weapons from Fallout. But I'm most inspired by modern robotic prototypes and real-life robots.

WHAT WOULD YOU SAY ARE THE FEATURES OF YOUR WORK?

I like to create robots and mechanicals. In my projects I try to depict a reality close to an engineering perspective.

1
—
2

1 *Foundry Train*
2 *Cover of Train*

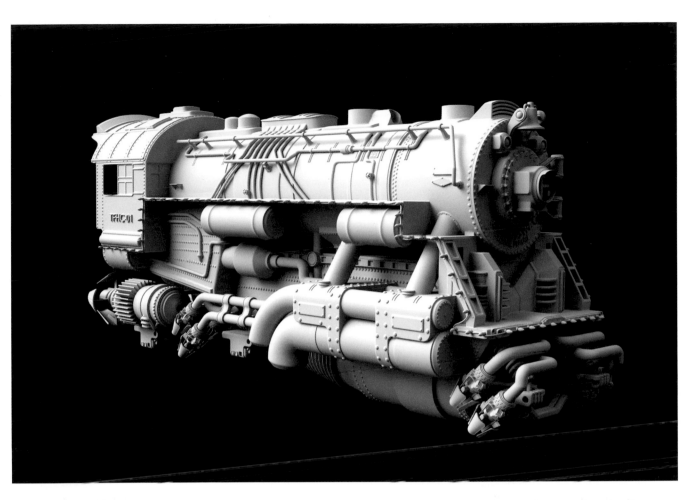

1

1 *Foundry Express Final*

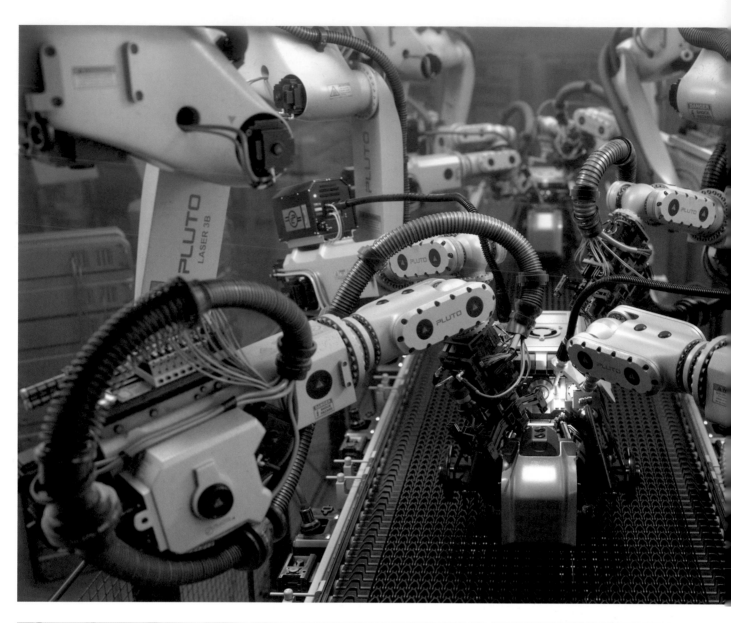

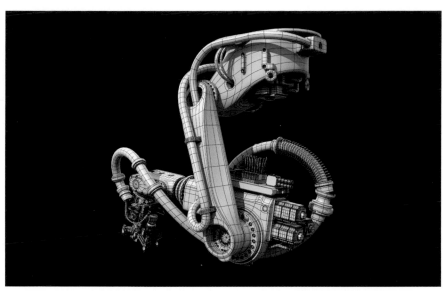

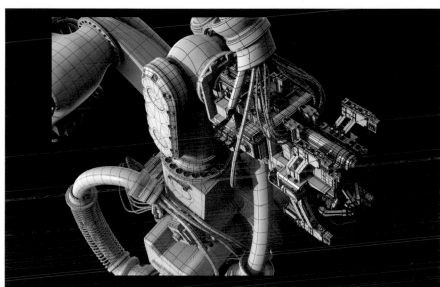

1 *Robotic Arms Final*

2 *Robotic Arms Wip Clay*

3 *Arm Side Wireframe with Alfachannel*

4 *Arm Top Front Wireframe with Alfachannel*

DASIIOGIKS

ABOUT THE ARTIST: Tian Guo (AKA Dasiiogiks) graduated from the Sculpture Department of Luxun Academy of Fine Arts, and has worked in art education for more than six years. He has a wide range of hobbies and subjects of study, including animals, weapons, cars, psychology, the universe and life, etc. He says he is used to the monotony of the pencil, and when using software, he draws some basic technology, but often forgets to build the layer, so he is not as good at software applications as he always wants to focus on the painting itself.

MATERIALS AND TOOLS: Pencil and hand painting board

ARTIST WEBSITE: artstation.com/artist/dasiiogiks

WHEN DID YOU START CREATING MECHANICAL DESIGNS? WHAT WAS YOUR OPPORTUNITY TO START?

I liked to secretly design things starting from primary school, mainly because it was not easy to watch cartoons when I was a child. Often I couldn't satisfied, so I drew them myself.

OF THE SEVERAL TYPES OF MECHANIC DESIGNS, WHAT DO YOU THINK ARE THE DIFFERENCES BETWEEN THEM? WHICH ARTISTS OR ART FORMS HAVE INFLUENCED YOUR CREATIONS?

I think it is necessary to take a person's understanding and cognition of the real world as a starting point, and to set an end in the future or in the past when a mechanical setting appears. The difference can be found in my works. Since I was a sculpture major in college, Michelangelo, Giacometti, Duchamp, Menzel and others are all my favorite artists, and they influence me all the time.

AS A CONCEPT ARTIST, HOW DO YOU PREPARE FOR A NEW WORK? WHAT ARE THE NECESSARY PRINCIPLES?

I'm not a professional mechanical concept designer—I just try to draw things out of my imagination occasionally. I think machinery is usually produced at a production plant, and has a certain universality, so the setting of the machine will naturally reflect the production situation at that time, with the view of the world at that time; so the appropriate or contradictory elements will stand out. In terms of preparation, I think many materials will influence the space for independent thinking, and I try to figure out the ideas behind some classical designs, which is also beneficial.

1

1 *Sketch*
Painted this many years ago. Originally I wanted to draw a Hummer also want to draw a robot, and then get this work

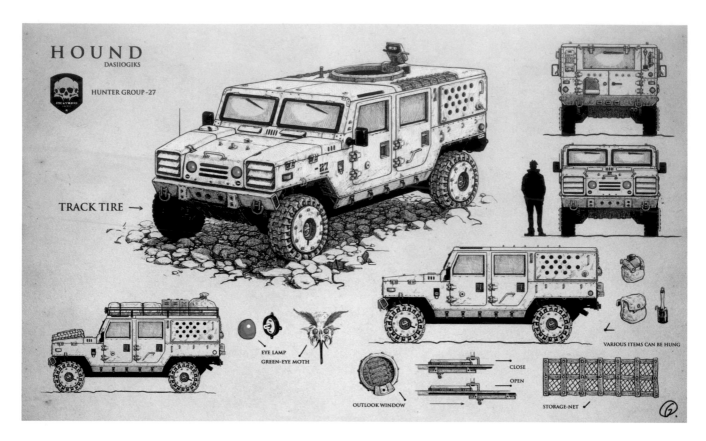

HOUND DASIIOGIKS

HUNTER GROUP-27

TRACK TIRE →

EYE LAMP
GREEN-EYE MOTH

VARIOUS ITEMS CAN BE HUNG

OUTLOOK WINDOW

CLOSE
OPEN

STORAGE-NET

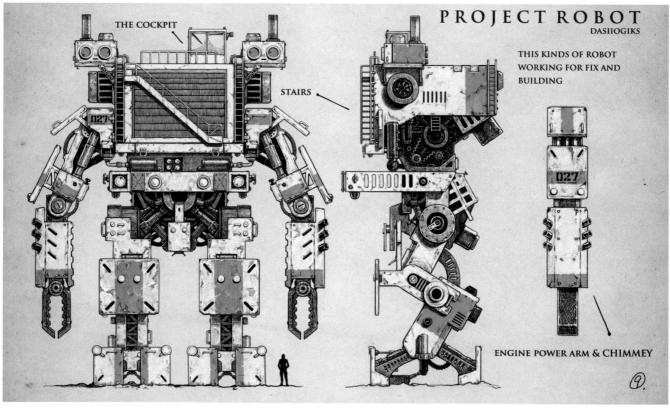

THE COCKPIT

STAIRS

PROJECT ROBOT DASIIOGIKS

THIS KINDS OF ROBOT
WORKING FOR FIX AND
BUILDING

ENGINE POWER ARM & CHIMMEY

1 | 3
2 |

1 Hound
A cross-country car from an original story, used by land-infected human hunters, re-formed from the remnants of a prehistoric war

2 Project Robot
An engineering robot from an original story, used for construction and handling by land-infected humans, re-formed from the remnants of a prehistoric war

3 Sketch
Based on a car and a robot

SOME DRAFT[...]
DASIIOGIKS

moon
史前空中城市
漂游岛
忍

From an original story that include: a lunar ark used by prehistoric humans for migrating to another planet; a "sky city" after nuclear war; an elephant variation after the war; abandoned soldiers; mutants and giant robots

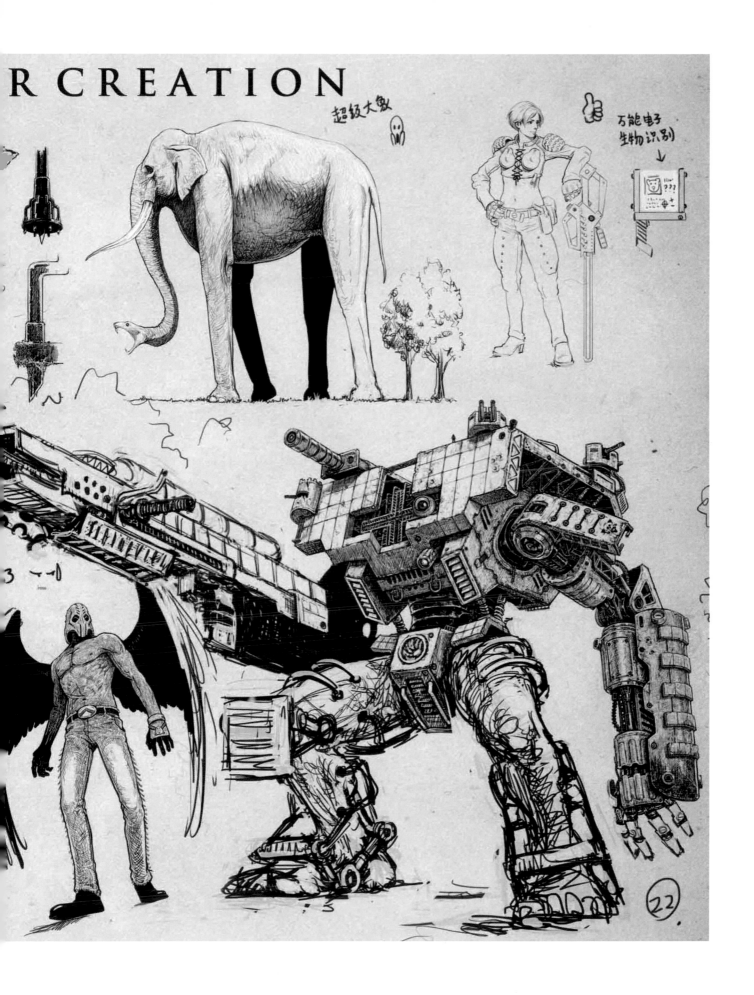

R CREATION

超级大象

万能电子
生物识别

LORENZ HIDEYOSHI RUWWE

ABOUT THE ARTIST: Lorenz Hideyoshi Ruwwe is a freelance concept artist and illustrator who works for clients in the entertainment business, including filmmakers, authors, game developers and private individuals.
MATERIALS AND TOOLS: Photoshop, Blender and Modo
ARTIST WEBSITE: https://www.artstation.com/hideyoshi

WHEN DID YOU START CREATING MECHANICAL DESIGNS? WHAT WAS YOUR OPPORTUNITY TO START?

I think my earliest influences came from Japanese mangakas who depicted mecha designs in their stories—even Dragon Ball, for example. More prominently Otomo. But those didn't really make me try to draw machines. A bit later, when I was 16 years old, I found Feng Zhu's old industrial designs done in ink and marker and was so impressed with them that I wanted to try those myself.

WHAT TOOLS AND MATERIALS DO YOU PREFER? WHAT ARE THEIR FEATURES AND HOW DO THEY HELP YOU WITH YOUR WORK?

I mostly work digital nowadays, in Photoshop and 3D programs. When I design spacecraft for a book cover for example, I like to create them directly in 3D like I am using Legos to build something. It's like model kit making. Then you can arrange them in a scene with other elements and light them before rendering them. Because 3D has become so powerful, it's a lot like being a director of photography, choosing your light setup, camera lenses and angles to see what works best to tell your story. And when you shout "action," the computer starts to render the scene! I also still like using good old pencil and ink or markers to draw on paper. Digital tools can make you lazy because you can correct anything you want. So using traditional media helps you to stay sharp and disciplined with your art.

WHAT WOULD YOU SAY ARE THE FEATURES OF YOUR WORK? HOW DO YOU FIND AND DEEPEN YOUR OWN STYLE?

I think it's most important to let the style find you and not the other way around. It will come out naturally if you don't try to force it into something else. I also started out copying other artists. It can help in the beginning as you learn to draw, I guess. At some point you have to embrace your individual artistry and stick with it. If I had to characterize my own work (which is hard), I could say that I try for it to be neat and tidy but at the same time also make it appear effortless. I like clarity and looseness. The outcome is always best when it flows out naturally.

AS A CONCEPT ARTIST, HOW DO YOU PREPARE FOR A NEW WORK? WHAT ARE THE NECESSARY PRINCIPLES?

It's important to understand the clients' wishes and address them. Engage with them and ask questions to get a good grasp of what they are looking for. Then as you progress with the work, keep asking for feedback and help elevate the work with your experience and skills.

1 1 *Millennium Falcon*
Fanart for which I experimented with 3D vegetation and a vibrant color scheme

1   2
    3

1 *Purple Spacecraft*

     A book cover illustration for Michael Wallace's Queen of the Void trilogy of novels

2 *Arch*

     A 30-minute speed painting

3 *Visitors*

     For this piece I tried to create as much as possible in 3D, with additional

     photobashing

1   1 *Legend of Galactic Heroes*
     Commissioned fanart illustration for Legends of Galactic Heroes, showing Brunhild and Barbarossa over the planet Odin

ALEKSANDR LANKOV

ABOUT THE ARTIST: Aleksandr Lankov is a designer, artist and architect living in Penza, Russia. He strives for and hopes to have a unique design style.

MATERIALS AND TOOLS: Pencil, Ink, Paper and Cardboard

ARTIST WEBSITE: https://www.behance.net/alx941
https://vk.com/alx941
https://www.instagram.com/alx941/
https://www.talenthouse.com/alx941

WHAT TOOLS AND MATERIALS DO YOU PREFER? WHAT ARE THEIR FEATURES AND HOW DO THEY HELP YOU WITH YOUR WORK?

You don't need to listen to this type of advice. As a corollary, the more work you do, the simpler your choices get. Rephrasing Leonardo of the North, you'll need a piece of rolled paper and a box: grab the closest more-or-less flat surface at hand and you'll find your own magical orb soon enough. A great deal has been said about selecting tools; probably my favourites are a pencil, a gel or an ink-pen.

WHICH MECHANICAL DESIGN FROM A GAME OR MOVIE IS YOUR FAVORITE?

Horror, supernatural and sci-fi movies of all sorts from the period of the 60s-90s.

CAN YOU SHARE WITH US YOUR EXPERIENCE OF CREATING THIS KIND OF WORK?

A lack of time for creative work will make you postpone your drawing, until the right time comes along, or you read an article on time shortage, and from that point you decide to draw no less than fifteen minutes per day. You'll find out you can draw every day, and at some point your "Work One" will show up, and that will inspire you to do your "Work Two," then "Drawing Three," then "Painting Four."

WHAT ARE YOUR PLANS FOR THE FUTURE IN MECHANICAL DESIGN?

Any painter would swiftly turn to deception if they said the only point of the drawings is the pleasure of real art discovery. Definitely, like any true artist, you want your paintings to be marveled at, collecting "SOLD" bur-marigolds, this way you can see the reason for your own path through life.

1

1 *The Whole Essence of the World*

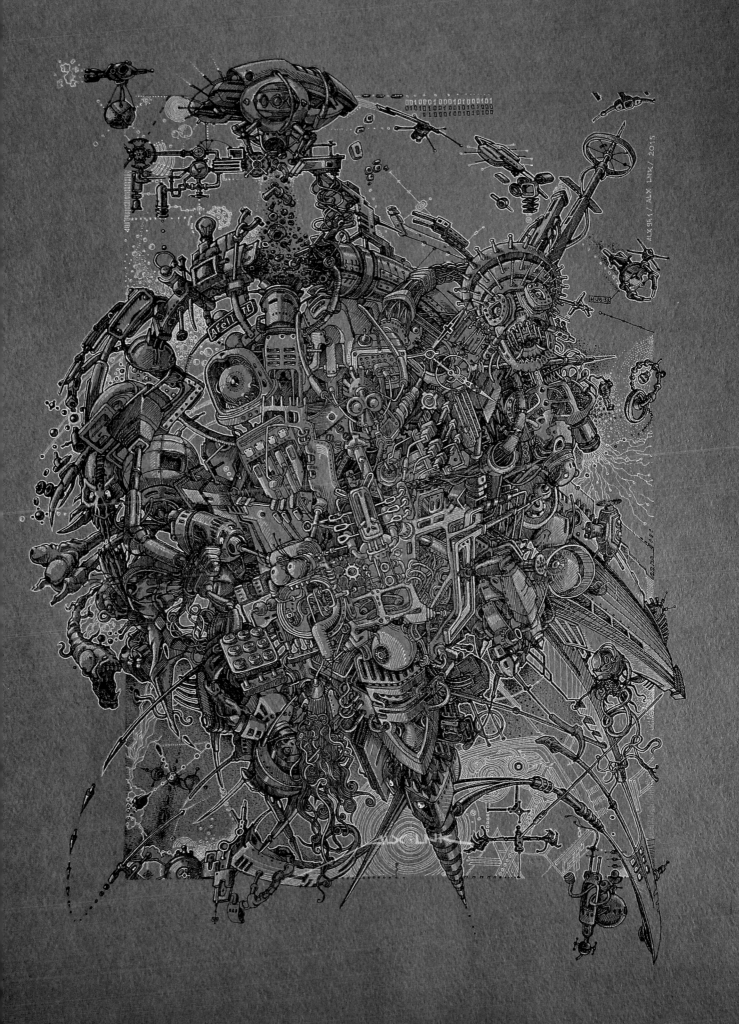

The Rise Of Darkness

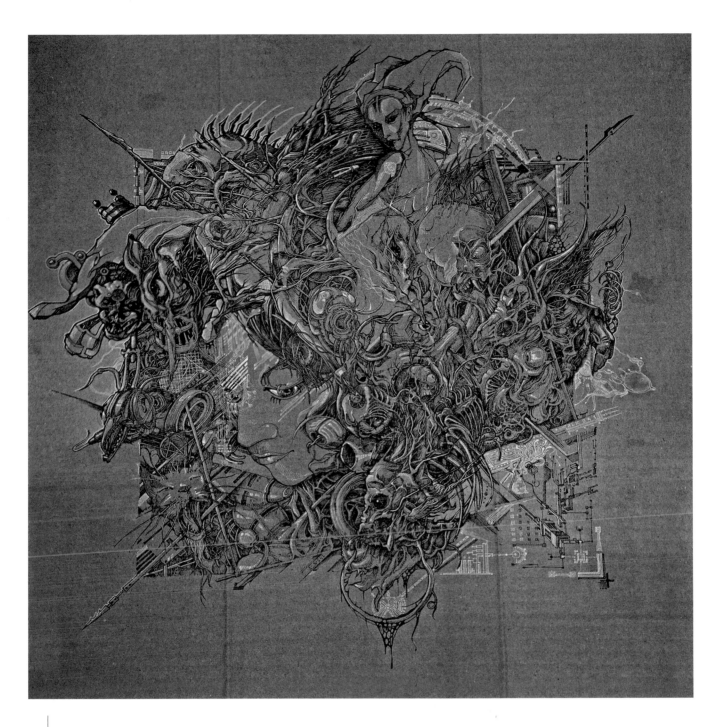

1 | 2

Collisions

por todas partes en todo sentido de la palabra
lo que necesitas
Hasta el final
por si acaso   desde cero

1

1 *From Scratch*

1   *The Life of Insects*

2   *Observers*

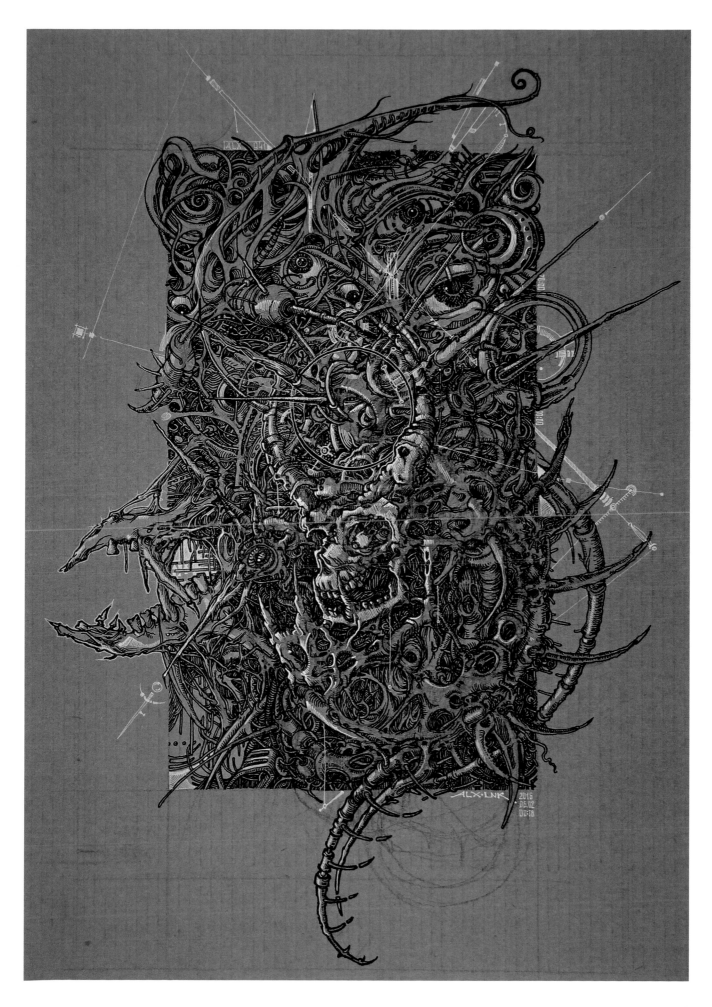

Machine Rendering II: The Book of Iron

Author: Dopress Books
Commissioning Editors: Guo Guang, Zeng Sheng
English Editors: Xu Xu, Song Pei
Copy Editor: Jennifer Fossenbell
Book Designer: Qiu Hong

©2018 by China Youth Press, Roaring Lion Media Co., Ltd. and CYP International Ltd. China Youth
Press, Roaring Lion Media Co., Ltd. and CYP International Ltd. have all rights which have been
granted to CYP International Ltd. to publish and distribute the English edition globally.

First published in the United Kingdom in 2018 by CYPI PRESS

Add: 79 College Road, Harrow Middlesex, HA1 1BD, UK
Tel: +44 (0) 20 3178 7279
E-mail: sales@cypi.net editor@cypi.net
Website: www.cypi.net
ISBN: 978-1-908175-80-9
Printed in China